· TROPHIES ·

ALL ABOARD

Harcourt

Orlando   Boston   Dallas   Chicago   San Diego

Visit *The Learning Site!*
www.harcourtschool.com

Photo Credits

(t) = top, (b) = bottom, (c) = center, (l) = left, (r) = right, (bkgd) = background.

Page: 100 Eric M. White; 107 The Granger Collection, New York; 110-116, Corbis; 206-207 Douglas Peebles/Corbis; 207 Ted Streshinsky/Corbis; 208-209 George Hall/Corbis; 209 Roger Ressmeyer/Corbis; 210 Gary Braasch/Corbis; 210-211 Paul A. Souders/Corbis; 212 Michael S. Yamashita/Corbis; 214 Bettman/Corbis; 219 Ralph White/Corbis; 220 Christie's Images/Corbis; 221 Bettmann/Corbis; 222-228 NASA.

Illustration Credits

Page: 13, 53, 149, 189, 213, Joe Boddy; 69, 133, 229, Toni Caldwell; 21, 93, 109, 173, Doron Putka.

Printed in the United States of America

ISBN 0-15-325343-6

3 4 5 6 7 8 9 10   039   10 09 08 07 06 05 04 03 02

CONTENTS

Dig In and Win 6
by Sydnie Meltzer Kleinhenz

[Teacher Read-Aloud] News Shorts 13

The Tea Boat 14
by Deborah Akers

[Teacher Read-Aloud] Tea Enters, Tea Leaves 21

Expectations 22
by Phyllis Root

The Little Big Champion 30
by Nelson Morales

Saving Town Garden 38
by Lisa Eisenberg

The Portrait 46
by Dave McCluskie

[Teacher Read-Aloud] Early American Schoolbooks 53

Finding Queen 54
by Deborah Akers

Possum Grins 62
by Sharon Fear

[Teacher Read-Aloud] Ludicrous Limericks 69

Floatplane Rescue 70
by Kaye Gager

The Johnstown Flood 78
by Kana Riley

Iceman of the Alps **86**
by Deborah Eaton

Teacher Read-Aloud **Merry Mix-Ups** **93**

It's a Wonder! **94**
by Susan M. Fischer

Treasures of the Pharaoh **102**
by Doris Licameli

Teacher Read-Aloud **Archaeo-Jokes** **109**

Vesuvius: A.D. 79 .... **110**
by John Reed

The Wisdom of Jefferson **118**
by Meish Goldish

Follow the Wild Geese **126**
by Ron Gellar

Teacher Read-Aloud **Daffynitions** **133**

Music in the Air **134**
by Pam Zollman

Invented by Mistake **142**
by William Bailey

Teacher Read-Aloud **Cook's Comedy** **149**

Honorable Mention **150**
by Edward Cruz

Making Freedom's Bell **158**
by Lee Chang

A Summer Treat **166**
by Marco Antunez

Teacher Read-Aloud **Define It!** **173**

Heather's Farm Summer **174**
by Kathryn Corbett

A Friend in Need **182**
by Jennifer Lien

Teacher Read-Aloud **Our Best Friend** **189**

Sitting It Out **190**
by Mel Vincent

The Cowboy's Catalog **198**
by Caren B. Stelson

Great Shakes! **206**
by Meish Goldish

Teacher Read-Aloud **Pick the Right One** **213**

Finding the Titanic **214**
by Meish Goldish

Mission Possible **222**
by Susan M. Fischer

Teacher Read-Aloud **That's What He Said!** **229**

Untangling the Web **230**
by Caren B. Stelson

Cindy "Science" Spots the Clues . . . **238**
by Mary Wright

Dig In and Win

by Sydnie Meltzer Kleinhenz
illustrated by Cathy Diefendorf

Pinerock BMX Club - June

Samantha was doing well in the BMX Club's June ride. She had pedaled over several bumps in the track without tipping her bike. Now she sped up a slope and popped off the hill for a jump—and crash-landed! There went all hope of a win this time. Looking glum, she got up, dusted off her pants, and picked up her bike.

Zack, a kid she knew from past rides, ran onto the track to help her. "Are you all right?" he asked.

When she nodded, he grinned. "That was some wipe-out!" he commented.

Samantha blushed crimson from embarrassment. "Thanks for the compliment," she joked. "I really want to get into the Pinerock Club, but that isn't how to do it!"

"Maybe BMX riding isn't for you," Zack said.

"It is, too!" Samantha huffed. "If I just had a track close to home, I could be good at it. I'd ride all the time and work on my skills. Then you'd see some quality riding."

Going home, Samantha puzzled over how she could get good at BMX skills. When she rode on ramps or jumped over plants, adults got upset. They said things like "You can't ride there!" and "Cut that out!"

Close to home, her dad drove past the trash-filled lot that belonged to Mr. Jones. Samantha stared at its dips and bumps. "Dad! Look what I see!" she said.

"What do you see?" her dad asked, curious.

"Well, if Mr. Jones will let us use his lot, I see a BMX track right close to home!" she said, filled with optimism.

"Now, that's being resourceful," said her dad. "It was shrewd of you to see that."

At home, Samantha rushed to ask Mr. Jones if she could make his lot into a BMX track. She was thrilled when he said yes to her plan. Then she asked several friends to help her. They all admired her plan and shared her optimism.

Five kids came over with rakes, spades, and hoses. They attached the hoses in a long line out Samantha's back gate and down the lane to the lot.

"Very inventive!" Samantha's mom commented.

The kids smiled. Then they pulled on plastic gloves and grabbed big trash bags. It was time to tackle the task of getting rid of the trash.

Next, the kids planned their track. They raked it flat here and piled up hills there. Then they used the spades to make bumps and dips.

The job lasted a long time. Some adults who passed by said the kids wouldn't finish it. Some stopped and admired Samantha's enterprising plan. Curious kids came to look and then to help.

At last the track was finished. All the kids helped hose it down to stop the dust from drifting. That was fun on a hot day! Then they yelled to Samantha, "Speech! Speech!"

Samantha lifted her hands and said, "Fantastic job! Thanks for all your help. Now, let's ride!" The kids were quick to line up with their bikes.

With a track so close to home, all the kids' skills got very good. At Pinerock's next ride, it was not just Samantha who was invited into the club. Several of her friends were, too. Samantha liked that!

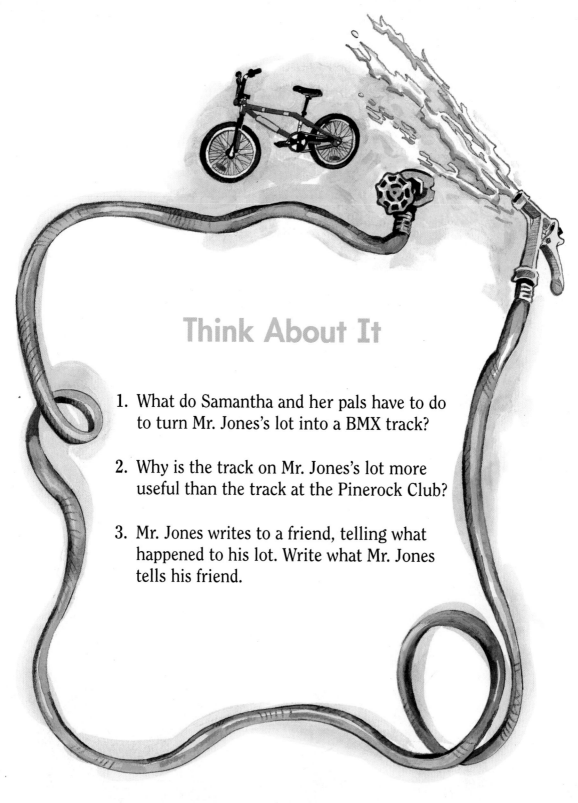

Think About It

1. What do Samantha and her pals have to do to turn Mr. Jones's lot into a BMX track?

2. Why is the track on Mr. Jones's lot more useful than the track at the Pinerock Club?

3. Mr. Jones writes to a friend, telling what happened to his lot. Write what Mr. Jones tells his friend.

News Shorts

A baboon has disappeared from the city zoo. Officials suspect monkey business.

A cargo plane carrying a load of boomerangs had mechanical trouble soon after take-off. It returned to the airport ten times.

The Rod and Reel Club reports a decline in the number of trout in area rivers this year. Scientists fish for an explanation.

Citizens complain about motorized baby carriages. The noise is driving them buggy.

13

The Tea Boat

by Deborah Akers   **illustrated by Jacqueline Rogers**

Len ran down the dock. The Yees' fishing boat was coming in from the sea. He could see Mr. Yee on the deck. Was he unaccompanied? No, there was Mrs. Yee, tipping a tub over the side.

"Oh, no, not again," said Len. "A new leak, Mr. Yee?" He grabbed the rope to lead the rig in to the dock.

Mr. Yee nodded. The fish in the boat had attracted a flock of gulls. Their antics were hilarious, but the Yees did not smile.

Len helped the Yees home with the fish.

Mrs. Yee said, "At least we got two big nets of fish. We will make money on that." She went to get them a snack.

"We sprung a leak again. We cannot keep this up!" said Mr. Yee. This sulkiness was not like him.

Len spoke up. "You will not be safe at sea until the leak is fixed."

Mrs. Yee set down some tea and honey cakes. The sweet steam of the tea made Len feel good.

Len clapped his hands. "Your tea and honey cakes are the best!" Mrs. Yee smiled at his applause.

"We can fix the leak again," said Mr. Yee. "Then the same thing could happen the next time we go out. In the past, we have had much success with this boat. Now it is too old, and we are getting too old to fish!"

"You will have success again," Len said. Inside, he did not know how. Things did not seem promising.

Len drank some tea and ate a bite of cake. He had to think. Then, as he ate, it came to him! He leaped up and hugged Mrs. Yee. "The tea and cakes!" he said.

Mr. and Mrs. Yee looked at Len. What did he mean?

"Mr. Yee, we need to seal that leak. Mrs. Yee, you must bake a big batch of honey cakes. Make a big jug of your hot tea, too! Then we will all meet at the dock when the sun comes up."

The Yees trusted Len, so they did as he said.

The sun came up on Len and the Yees in the old boat. The leak was sealed, the honey cakes were stacked, and a big jug of tea sat by their feet.

"Where are we going with all of this?" said Mr. Yee.

"You will see," said Len as he sped the boat to the shopping arcade. They could hear the noise of the vendors. Len docked the boat in the middle of it all.

Then Len set out the cakes and tea with a flourish.

"Rest your feet at the Tea Boat," he yelled over the noise.

The sweet smell attracted an audience. It was a novelty to eat cakes with tea on a fishing boat. The line grew long, and the snacks went fast.

"We will be back," said Len.

Applause and cheers rang out for the Tea Boat.

"Your old fishing boat seems quite promising now," said Len. The Yees grasped his hands and smiled. They had to agree!

Think About It

1. What problem do the Yees have? How does Len solve it?

2. The author says that the Yees trust Len. Why do you think they trust a young boy so much?

3. The Yees want to advertise the Tea Boat so they will have more customers. Create an ad for them to place in the newspaper.

Tea Enters . . . Tea Leaves

How about a nice cup of *cha*? That's the word for *tea* in Mandarin Chinese. According to legend, Emperor Shen-Nung of China discovered the tea leaf by accident about 3,000 years ago. The story says that he was boiling his drinking water when the wind blew some leaves from a tea plant into the water. The emperor liked the result, and tea drinking was born. We get the word *tea* from the Amoy Chinese word *te*, the Malay *the*, and the Dutch *thee*.

Coffee drinkers? They need to perk up.

Describe the water supply? It's pretty clear.

Grow peach trees? It's the pits.

Pick oranges? It's very appealing.

Make maple syrup? Don't be a sap.

Raise corn? Aw, shucks.

Grow cabbage? You're sure to get ahead.

Know a locksmith? That's the key question.

Hot-tempered green vegetables? They're always getting steamed.

EXPECTATIONS

by Phyllis Root • **illustrated by Jim Darnell**

When I was in school in the 1960s, sports were for boys. Boys had teams and managers. Boys had letter jackets. Boys got to play for a trophy and win medals. There were lots of expectations for boys.

We girls got to sit on the sidelines and cheer them on. Oh, we could play kickball at lunchtime in grade school. We could play baseball at home. I had to bat left-handed so my team wouldn't win all the time. But *real* sports? For girls, there were no teams, no managers, no medals, no trophy. For girls, there were no expectations at all.

From seventh grade on, we didn't even have time to play kickball at lunch. All we had were P.E. classes. Sometimes we played basketball. I could stand on the line and sink ten out of ten shots. Sometimes we played baseball. One time when I pitched, I struck out the entire team with my fastball. Everyone glared at me. Girls weren't supposed to be *that* good. I wasn't upset because I knew I had done a good job of pitching.

When John F. Kennedy became President, he wanted all kids to be fit. He made up a fitness test in which we would run and jump and do pull-ups and push-ups. If we did well enough on these tasks, we would get a neat patch.

We all made pledges of what we would do. I pledged to run very fast, jump several feet, and be a victor on the day of the fitness test.

My long jump was the longest in my class. I did lots of sit-ups and pull-ups. I trotted around the track for the run-walk. I was all set to be in the top group.

All that was left was the dash. I was tall and had long legs, and I ran fast. I was at my peak and favored to win. I wanted to do well for the President and for the U.S.A.

The teacher yelled "Go!" And I shot off down the track. When I was almost to the finish line, I tripped and fell. I stumbled across the finish line, my leg bleeding. Friends came running to console me.

My time wasn't good, and my leg was too sore from my fall to run again. Maybe, just maybe, all the rest of my scores would be good enough. I still had expectations of winning that beautiful patch.

When the teacher called the names of those who had won patches, we all clapped and yelled. Then she called the names of the kids who had come close. I was one of them.

"If you had worked a little harder," the teacher said to us, "you would have won patches, too."

I looked at my scab, all the memento I had of the President's fitness test. I acted as if I were immune to what the teacher said, but I wasn't. I had not met her expectations, and I felt that I had let the President down.

By the time there were sports teams for girls, I was out of school. Now I watch my girls play on their school teams, and I cheer for them as hard as I can.

I still play sports, but I've found something else I like to do, too. It needs no trophy or medal or manager. I set my expectations for myself, and I am a victor every time I do it.

I write.

Note: Phyllis Root has written many books for children, including *Aunt Nancy and Old Man Trouble* and *Aunt Nancy and Cousin Lazybones*.

Think About It

1. What did the writer want to do when she was in school?

2. How do you think the writer felt about President Kennedy?

3. Think about what you learned about Phyllis Root, the writer of this story. Make a web with words that describe her. Use your web to help you write a descriptive paragraph about Phyllis Root.

The Little BIG Champion

by Nelson Morales   illustrated by Lindy Burnett

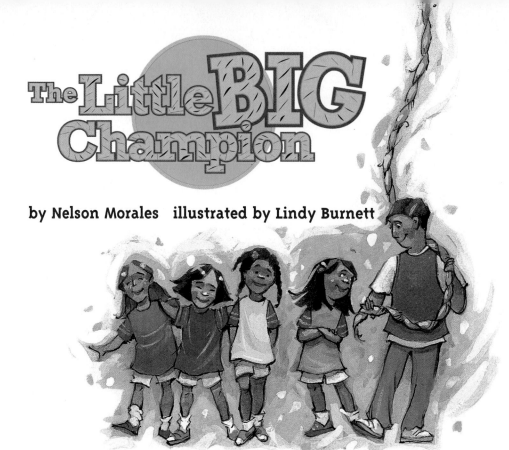

"All of you will go up the rope," Mr. Parks, our sixth-grade P.E. teacher, said. "Please line up five to a rope."

My friend Carmen got in line reluctantly. "I know I can't go up the rope," she said.

"You will all be able to do it," Mr. Parks said. "It just takes time and hard work. We'll be on the ropes for several weeks. As you strengthen your arms and legs, you will begin to make progress."

"For several weeks!" the class fumed. "What happened to basketball? You said we could play."

"Indeed you will!" our teacher said. "When each of you is a champion on the ropes, we'll start on basketball. In the meantime, let's stop the commotion and get to work."

There was nothing for it but to make going up the ropes our job. We went at it in our free time, pushing ourselves until exhaustion hit.

The teacher assigned us rope mates, and Carmen was assigned to work with me. We made an odd team because I'm big and she's little.

"You'll see, Carmen—we're going to be the stars of the ropes," I said to her.

Carmen didn't share my optimism. To be accurate, she didn't have a bit of optimism. Still, she stuck to the task of strengthening her arms and legs. I had to admire her. I said she had an instinct for hard work, if not for rope work. She smiled at the compliment.

At the end of two weeks, Mr. Parks rummaged in his backpack for his notes on our progress. After consulting them, he said, "You're all making good progress. I'm very pleased and impressed, and I hope you are, too. In a week we'll have a contest to see which team is the fastest."

"Carmen and I will win," I called out. I must admit that I like to brag—it's a weakness of mine.

"Big talk, Jane!" someone yelled back. "We'll be your opponents, you know!"

"TIME will be your opponent," Mr. Parks said. "I'll time each one of you going up and down the rope. The team with the best combined time will win."

At home, I happened to make a comment about the
upcoming contest. My dad and mom were curious.

"How do you start up the rope, Jane?" Dad asked.

"First, I jump and grab the rope as far up as I can. Then,
with my legs flexed, I grip it between my feet. When I've
started up, Carmen takes the rope and keeps it in line for me.
I do the same for her when we switch. We each have to do our
part."

"How do you win the contest?" Mom wanted to know.

"Mr. Parks will time each of us with his stopwatch," I said. "The team with the best combined time will win."

"Will you each know your time?" my dad asked.

"No," I said, "we'll just get team times."

Dad got out his stopwatch. "For fun, you can use this to time yourself and check your progress," he said. "It's accurate, but keep your time to yourself. It's not necessary to brag!"

I nodded. With the watch, I could compete with my own time for going up and down the rope. This was going to be fun!

In a week we were as ready as we were going to get. Mr. Parks held the contest, clicking his stopwatch as we went up and down. He made a note of each team's time.

When Carmen and I went, I put on a real push and sped up the rope. I timed myself, but I didn't check Dad's watch. I could look at it on my way home.

When the winning team was named, Carmen and I were the victors. We were the stars of the ropes, just as I had predicted!

When the commotion ended, the teacher congratulated us. "You two went up and down in 58 seconds. Your time was the best by two seconds!"

35

Carmen and I were the champions! On the way home, Carmen said to me, "Jane, you were the big champion."

I got out my dad's stopwatch. My time had been 30 seconds. So Carmen's time was 28 seconds.

"Carmen, YOU'RE the big champion!" I said. I let her see the watch. "You beat my 30 seconds. You may be little, but you were the best of all!"

Carmen grinned with pride. "How about that!" she said. "I'm the little big champion!"

Think About It

1. Which team has the best combined time for going up and down the ropes? How long does it take each girl to go up and come back down?

2. How do you think Jane feels at first about being assigned to work with Carmen on the ropes? How do you think her feelings change?

3. Mr. Parks is asked to write up his notes about the rope project. He is to explain why he assigned it, what the class learned from it, and how everyone liked it. Write the notes he hands in.

Saving Town Garden

by Lisa Eisenberg   illustrated by Lisa Carlson

Joanie pulled up a weed. "Let's go, Mom!" she called. "We've done enough for today. I'm tired."

Joanie and her mom had been working at their plot in Town Garden. A lot of their meals came from what they planted there.

"Okay, honey, just wait till I finish picking these peas," Joanie's mom said.

Joanie looked up. "Those two men were here again today. Did you find out what they want?"

"I did, Joanie. It seems those men don't like Town Garden. They're making an issue of our using the land this way. They went to Town Hall and dug up an ordinance—a rule," Joanie's mom explained. "They claim it's a violation to have a garden on this block. It's going to be our job to find new land and move all our plants."

"I think that's just an excuse," Joanie grumbled, pulling off her gardening gloves. "I think they want to use the land for something else."

"Well, the decision has been made, Joanie," her mom said. "It's too late now to save Town Garden."

"Maybe it is," Joanie said to herself. "Then again, maybe it isn't."

The next day, Joanie talked to Callie and Jeff, friends whose families also had plots in Town Garden. The three went to the library and asked Mr. Adair for help. With his aid, they found the ordinance they were looking for.

"The men are right," Jeff said after they looked through it. "We can't save our garden."

"It's hard to beat an ordinance," Mr. Adair agreed.

Callie, Jeff, and Joanie started to leave, feeling glum. Then Joanie called out, "Wait!" On the library wall was a note that said *Town Meeting Next Week*.

"Maybe we could get the garden issue on the meeting's agenda," Joanie said. "Then we could ask for a vote on that ordinance!" said Joanie.

"Who's afraid of an ordinance?" Jeff joked, and their optimism rose again.

The three went back to Mr. Adair with their idea. "To get Town Garden on the agenda," he said, "it would be helpful to get an article in *The Times*."

Callie said to Joanie and Jeff, "I could interview you two. You could explain why we need our garden. Come on—let's go do it right now!"

"We get all of our greens from our garden," Jeff Conway explained. "Town Garden helps us eat right."

Joanie Chen claimed it's the same for her. "My mom's pay doesn't go far. The garden helps us out. Yes, the ordinance does say no gardens there, but we didn't know about it. Now we just want to save Town Garden!"

In two days, Callie's interview appeared in *The Times*. She ended her article with a call for people to attend a meeting at the library. They had all felt this would be an effective way to discuss the problem.

Joanie made a speech at the library meeting. "Save Town Garden!" she called over the applause at the end. "Who's afraid of an ordinance?"

At last, the day came for the Town Meeting. The men Joanie had seen at the garden spoke. "Town Garden is in violation of an ordinance. We need that land for a parking lot."

Joanie rose to her feet. "I ask that we all vote against the ordinance. Our town does need a parking lot, but the lot can be on any land. We can postpone a decision on that."

Town Hall was filled with applause. Then a man spoke. "The kids are right about your parking lot—it can go anywhere downtown. They've donated a lot of their time. I'll donate land for the lot, so you'll need no funding for it. Now there's no excuse for getting rid of Town Garden!"

When the votes came in, the decision was a win for Town Garden. The ordinance was voted down!

"We saved Town Garden!" Joanie exclaimed, her eyes sparkling. "I knew we could do it!" Joanie, Jeff, and Callie clapped their hands. "Let's hear it for Town Garden!" they all yelled.

Think About It

1. Why do Joanie, Callie, and Jeff want to save Town Garden?

2. Why does a man donate some land for a parking lot? What do you think would have happened if he had not donated the land?

3. The next day, a story about Town Garden is on the front page of *The Times*. Write that news story.

THE PORTRAIT

by Dave McCluskie

illustrated by David Poole

The year was 1775. Todd and his dog, Bud, were walking down the road not far from his home near Boston. Todd was thinking about his pa, who was missing after a battle with the British.

A weak moan came to him from a nearby clump of trees. Todd stopped, and Bud gruffed belligerently at the unexpected noise.

"Help!" someone called out. Then there was a gasp and a groan of pain. A man in a red jacket was leaning against a big oak tree. As Todd approached, he could see a deep cut on the man's throat.

Todd looked down at the man disdainfully. "You're a Redcoat!" he said. "Why would I come to your aid? You'll get no help from me!"

The Redcoat raised a weak hand. "Please!" he begged Todd in a croak. Then he fainted.

"I can't just ignore him and leave him here," Todd grumbled to himself, "but I know I can't lift him by myself. I'll have to go get Sis to help." It was a hard job, but at last he and Meg got the Redcoat home and into bed.

The Redcoat woke up while Meg was cleaning and tending to the cut on his throat.

"Where am I?" he asked in dismay. He struggled to sit up, but he was too weak and fell back onto the bed.

"Now, you just rest," Meg coaxed him soothingly. The Redcoat closed his eyes and fell asleep.

Exasperated, Todd said, "Meg, how can you help him? He's a Redcoat! He may have killed Yankees like us. Why, he may have killed Pa!"

"Now, you hush, Todd," said Meg. "We have no knowledge of where Pa is. For all we know, some Redcoat may be helping him right now!"

Just then someone outside yelled, "Is anyone home?" Todd and Meg looked at each other in dismay.

"Don't you say a thing!" Meg hissed to Todd. "Get rid of that red coat—fast!" Todd scrambled to stuff the coat under the bed.

Meg pulled the blanket up to the man's chin. "Come in!" she called.

Two men came in and said that they were looking for Redcoats.

"After that last battle, some of the Redcoats were too weak to get back to camp," the first man explained. "They may be hiding in these parts. These are dangerous times."

"And hiding Redcoats is a dangerous occupation," the second man commented.

Todd did not dare look up. He hoped they couldn't feel his tension.

The two men gazed at the man in the bed.

"Sick, is he?" one of them inquired. The tension in the air increased.

Meg was unwavering. "Yes," she said, "very sick, I'm afraid."

"Well, we'll be going then," the man said. "I hope your pa gets well." The men left.

"Why did he say that?" Todd asked. Then he saw Meg look up at the portrait of his pa on the wall.

"Oh! Now I see!" The hair, the proud chin in the portrait—they were a lot like the Redcoat's.

Todd felt proud. Without having any knowledge of it, his pa had saved the man's life. Maybe some Redcoat would do the same for his pa.

Think About It

1. What do the men want when they come to Todd's home? Why do they not suspect what Todd and Meg are doing?

2. At first Todd says, "You're a Redcoat! You'll get no help from me!" Why do you think Todd helps the man after all?

3. What do you think will happen when the Redcoat gets well? Write the rest of the story.

Early American Schoolbooks

It's a Great Land by Bea A. Patriot

Choosing Sides in the Revolution by R. U. Certain

Stand Up for Your Rights! by U. Kantoo

Disadvantages of Independence by B. N. Frank

Beating the Enemy by Wynn N. Grinn

Making a Quick Escape by Justin Time

Berries and Other Edibles: Living Off the Land
   by Eaton Wright

Preparing for a Long Winter by Will B. Cold

Finding Queen

by Deborah Akers
illustrated by Winson Trang

I woke in the dark, startled awake by a terrible wailing outside. Below my window, my big Lab, King, was barking in anguish. My alarm clock said it was not quite time to get up.

I slid the window up and felt a chill wind outside. Brrr! Fall was in the air. "What is it, old fellow?" I asked. "Why did you get me up?"

I reached down and scratched King's ears and gave him a pat. I could see that he was very upset about something. "Stay there," I said. "I'll be right out." I shut the window, got dressed, and put on my jacket.

Something wasn't right. King led me to the shed where he and Queen, my other Lab, sleep. To my surprise, there was no sign of Queen anywhere.

"King, where's Queen?" I asked. King jumped around me, whining. He seemed to be trying to tell me something, but I didn't know what it was.

Inside, Mom was making a big stack of pancakes for breakfast. "Mom, have you seen Queen?" I asked.

Mom looked up from the stove in surprise. "What are you doing up, Matt? It's not even six yet."

"King was outside my window, and his yelping woke me up. Mom, Queen isn't in the shed or anywhere around."

"Now, don't get upset, Matt," Mom said. "You know Queen doesn't go far on her own. She must be somewhere nearby."

"King's the one who's upset. He seems to be asking me to help him find her. Can I go look for her?"

"Matt, we need your help to finish bringing in the harvest," Mom said. "There could be snow today."

"What if something bad has happened to Queen?" I asked, dismayed.

"She'll be okay, Matt, but you can look until it's time to eat."

King and I looked everywhere. We followed Queen's familiar routine, checking each stop she would make. She was nowhere to be seen.

Then Dad was calling me to come inside. I clapped my hands and called King. "We'll look again when I finish helping," I promised him. He wavered for a second. It was clear that he wanted to run off, but he came with me.

Harvesting was a familiar routine, but today we were rushed. There were rows of beans to pick, carrots to pull, and pumpkins to cut. Snow would bring finality to the growing season.

While we worked, King kept running to the top of the hill. He'd stand there looking down into the valley beyond. He'd come back when Dad called him, but he seemed to feel a compulsion to be on that hilltop.

At long last we finished our harvest, and Dad said I could go. King and I dashed home and checked once again, but Queen still wasn't there. Mom gave me a hug and wished us luck finding her. Then King sped off, and I followed him up the big hill.

As we went, I checked around each bush and tree we passed. The finality that fall always brings was in the air. From the hilltop, I could see snow blowing over the expanse of the valley. I knew I had to make a decision—keep looking for Queen or beat the snow home.

"What do we do now, King?" I asked. Just then, a little yelp came up to us from a deep ravine below. King shot off down the steep slope.

"Wait for me!" I called. The big Lab could leap rocks and bushes with ease. I was slow, slipping and sliding down the slope. I scrabbled for bushes to grab onto.

At the bottom of the ravine, in a thicket of trees, was a vacant shed. Well, not quite vacant. When I looked inside, I gasped in disbelief. There lay Queen! Her right rear leg looked broken. I sat down beside her and petted her soft ears while King put his nose to hers.

"King, Queen needs help! Go get Dad!" I said. "The snow will be here in no time." King ran off to bring help.

Queen was in pain, but she licked my hand. I talked to her, telling her how King wouldn't rest until we found her. "You'll be all right now, Queen. Dad will know just what to do for you."

King was back in a flash. When Dad ran in after him, he was dusted with snow.

"That dog of yours just about dragged me here!" he puffed. "I could tell you had found Queen. How is she?"

"Her leg looks broken, Dad. How will we get her home?"

"I think I can lift her, but first we need to splint that leg." I grabbed two strong sticks from the floor of the shed and handed them to Dad. He worked fast.

Ready to go, Dad gave King an admiring pat. "You're quite a dog, King! You saved Queen's life."

I engulfed King in a big hug. "Queen and I owe you one, old fellow," I said.

Think About It

1. How does King find Queen and save her?

2. How can you tell that King and Queen are important to Matt and his family?

3. If King could talk, how would he describe what happened when he looked for—and finally found—Queen? Write what you think he would say.

POSSUM GRINS

by Sharon Fear

illustrated by Lauren Klementz-Harte

Each year in June, Bob and I spend two weeks on Grandma and Grandpa's farm. One slow day, we were all down at the creek with our fishing poles.

"Look over by that big oak tree, Bob," said Grandpa. "See that possum poking around there?"

"I see it," said Bob.

"I did a good deed for that possum one time," Grandpa said. "Now, each time she sees me, she thanks me again."

Bob was curious. "How do you know it's the same possum? What did you do to help her?" he asked.

"Well, I'll tell you," said Grandpa.

I looked over at Grandma, and she looked back at me and winked. Grandpa could spin some yarns, all right, and we were going to hear one now.

"I had come down here to the creek right after a dangerous storm," Grandpa began. "It had rained hard, and the creek was rising at a rapid rate. A strong, rowdy wind had torn many branches off the trees. In fact, I was standing right about here when a big **CRACK!** made me look up. And what do you think I saw?"

"What, Grandpa?" Bob was all ears.

63

"A big branch had snapped, and a big mama possum was clinging to the broken end," Grandpa said. "Her little possums were struggling on the falling branch. **SPLASH!** Into the creek they went.

"Poor little wet things! They were bobbing up and down like corks, all of them whimpering and trembling, trembling and whimpering. They were afraid, but they hung on as the branch was swept downstream.

"Above me, their mama was crying out to them. She was so frantic that I just had to do what I could to help her."

"I went charging along the shore of the creek, following the branch and looking for a shallow spot. I couldn't find a shallow part, so I just went lunging in—right up to my chest! I was soaked and freezing, needless to say."

"What happened next?" asked Bob.

"I pounced on that branch and grappled with it in the rowdy waves. At last I pushed it to that spot, right where that big rock wedges into the bank.

"I pulled myself out of the creek, dripping wet and chilled to the bone, and what did I see?"

"What, Grandpa, what?" It was clear that Bob was thrilled. His eyes were wide with expectation.

"There was that mama possum with her children safe on her back," Grandpa said. "She was romping on the grass and went off into the forest with them. I don't know why, but I yelled out, 'You could at least say thank you!'

"Well, she must have felt embarrassed to seem ungrateful. She stopped in her tracks, swung herself around, and gave me a big grin. You see, that's how a possum says thank you—with a grin.

"Now, watch how I know that's the same possum."

Grandpa clapped his hands, and the possum by the tree looked up at us. "See," he said with pride.

"She's grinning!" Bob exclaimed in amazement, very impressed. Grandma didn't say anything. Nor did I. Bob is still little, so his knowledge of many things is limited. One day, when he's seen as many possums as I have, he'll know that all possums grin!

Think About It

1. What does Grandpa say he did to help the possum?

2. How does Bob feel about Grandpa's yarn? How does Bob's big sister feel about it? How can you tell?

3. What do you think Bob says and does the next time he sees a possum? Write your ideas.

Ludicrous Limericks

There once was a possum from Porter
Who wished that her tail were much shorter.
    When she hung from the door,
    Her head bumped the floor,
And off fell her sons and her daughter.

Sign in at
Cy's Inn

Cy, a seagull who lived on the shore,
Found fishing a terrible bore.
    He moved to Berlin
    Where he opened an inn.
So, see? Cy's a seagull no more.

An old grizzly bear that I knew
Could always find something to do.
    When it bored him to go
    On a walk to and fro,
He reversed it, and walked fro and to.

Floatplane RESCUE

by Kaye Gager   illustrated by Dan Burr

Don Sheldon landed his floatplane next to the railroad tracks. A train had come in. He was surprised to see a big yellow boat aboard it. The boat was being taken off a flatcar.

Don walked over to a bunch of men dressed in drab green outfits. They were looking at a map.

Don greeted one man he knew. "Going fishing?" he joked.

The man smiled. "Hi, Don! We're going up the Susitna River to check out some sites," he said.

"The Susitna froze hard this year. It's just starting to melt," said Don. "It may still be impassable."

The man brushed off Don's comment. "Our boat will make it just fine."

"You may find it a grueling, perilous trip," Don said. The man did not seem to care.

Don said, "I'll be up and down the Susitna a lot this week. I'll check on you from time to time."

The next day, Don did not see the boat on the Susitna. Nor did he see it the day after that. He looked down at the freezing rapids with alarm. Could that boat survive such a rugged course?

Fearing the worst, he looked down at the rapids one more time. Then he yelled in dismay! Near the shore were scraps of yellow!

Don soared back over the spot. Yes, there along the shore were scraps of the yellow boat!

But where were the men? He hoped they had bailed out. Don did not waste any more time. He came up with a rescue plan.

Back and forth he took the plane along the Susitna, looking for the men. Don could hear the roar of the rapids. The men could not survive long in the perilous water. He must find them, and fast!

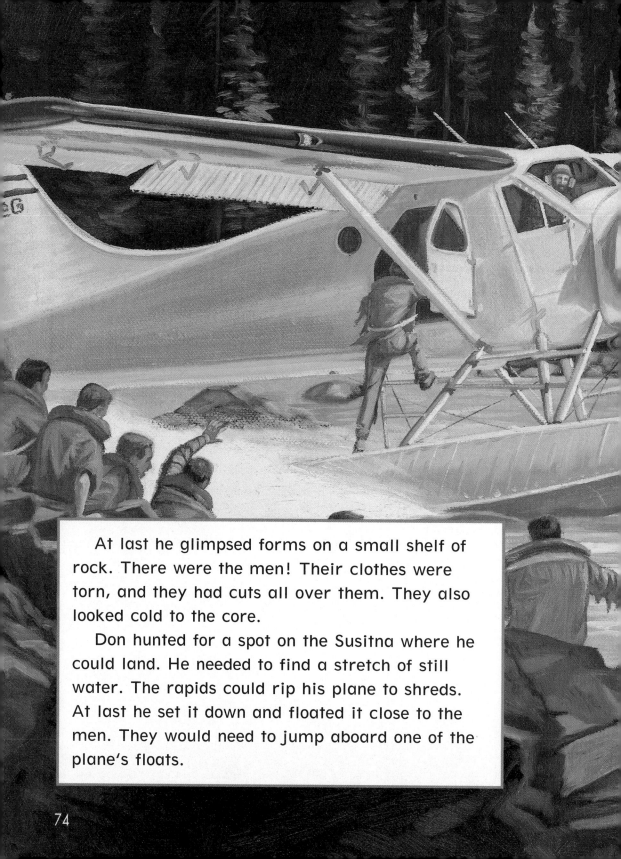

At last he glimpsed forms on a small shelf of rock. There were the men! Their clothes were torn, and they had cuts all over them. They also looked cold to the core.

Don hunted for a spot on the Susitna where he could land. He needed to find a stretch of still water. The rapids could rip his plane to shreds. At last he set it down and floated it close to the men. They would need to jump aboard one of the plane's floats.

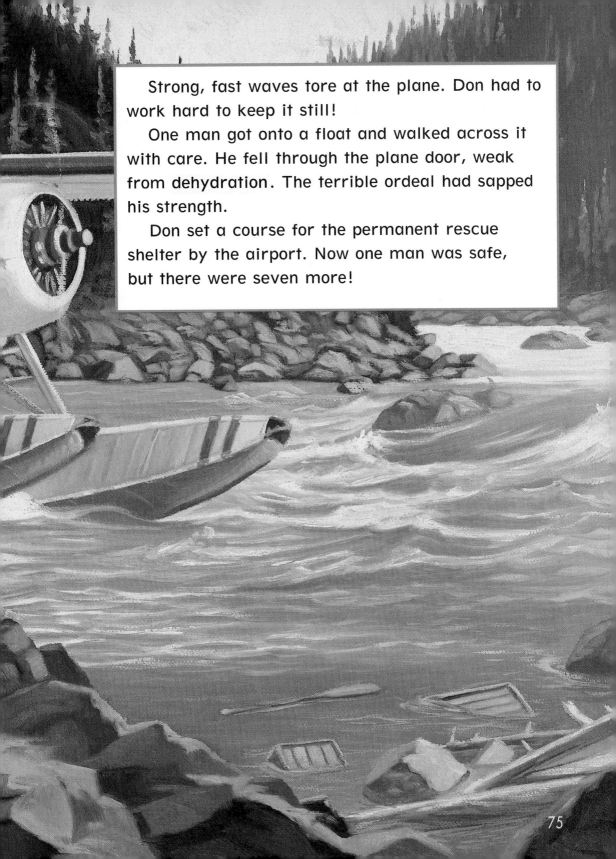

Strong, fast waves tore at the plane. Don had to work hard to keep it still!

One man got onto a float and walked across it with care. He fell through the plane door, weak from dehydration. The terrible ordeal had sapped his strength.

Don set a course for the permanent rescue shelter by the airport. Now one man was safe, but there were seven more!

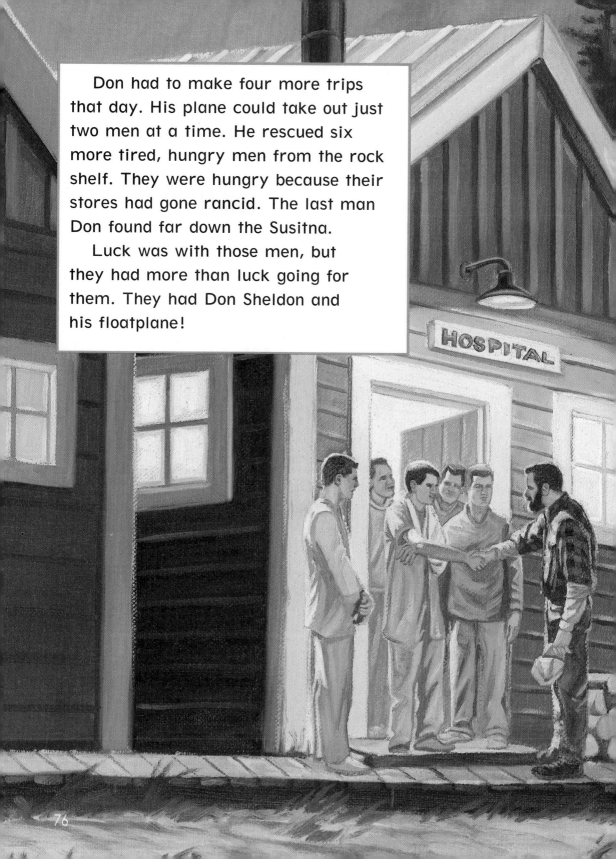

Don had to make four more trips that day. His plane could take out just two men at a time. He rescued six more tired, hungry men from the rock shelf. They were hungry because their stores had gone rancid. The last man Don found far down the Susitna.

Luck was with those men, but they had more than luck going for them. They had Don Sheldon and his floatplane!

Think About It

1. How was Don Sheldon able to save the men?

2. What feelings do you think Don Sheldon had while carrying out the rescue?

3. You are a writer for an Alaska paper. Write a news story about the rescue.

The Johnstown Flood

by Kana Riley

illustrated by Bob Dombrowski

Sixteen-year-old Victor Heiser pulled his coat around him. He leaped over puddles and wiped the rain from his eyes as he ran to the barn to do his chores.

It was just after 4:00 P.M. on May 31, 1889, in Johnstown, Pennsylvania. Rain had been coming down for two long days, and it didn't seem to be letting up.

Victor was alarmed to see that the barn was wet inside. Water was seeping in under the walls and doors. It lay in puddles on the floor.

Just then he heard a roar that awed him. It was like thunder, but it didn't stop. It seemed to be coming closer and closer.

Victor ran to the barn window to see where the noise was coming from. To his horror, a wall of water 30 feet tall was coming at him. In that instant, Victor realized what had happened. The old dam had broken at last! Then, before he had time to escape, the water lifted up the barn and swept it away.

Fourteen miles up the river from Johnstown was a big earth dam. It held back a large, human-made lake, or reservoir. With all the rain of the past two days, water in the lake had been rising all day.

By 3:10 P.M., the pressure of the water was getting dangerous. The old dam had not been well kept up. Now it could not take such pressure, and it broke. With a roar, the entire lake burst free. The water poured down toward Johnstown, flooding the river, its tributaries, and the valley.

Johnstown lay on a floodplain, yet its people weren't ready for a flood. They had not set up levees. Levees are strong walls that prevent damage in times of flood.

At 4:07 P.M., the river crested as tons of water came churning into Johnstown. The flood wiped out whatever was in its path. Stores, homes, barns, trains, cattle, and hundreds of people were swept into the swirling tide.

There was no time to raise an alarm. The water was coming too fast. People swam, grabbed tree branches to float on, or ran for the hills to escape the torrent.

Victor Heiser, trapped in his floating barn, scrambled onto its roof. There he held on for dear life as the barn rode one of the river's swift tributaries. He ended up in the town of Kernville, trembling and worn out but alive and safe.

The next day, June 1, people all around the United States learned about the Johnstown flood. The town had suffered a lot of damage, and people yearned to help. Volunteer workers, food, clothing, and dollars poured in.

In Washington, D.C., Clara Barton heard the news. She was the leader of the newly formed Red Cross. She and fifty doctors and nurses rushed to Johnstown. For the first time, the Red Cross set up shelters to take care of flood victims. They fed them and gave them somewhere to stay until their homes were fixed.

Rain fell on Johnstown for forty more days. Workers slogged around in deep mud, taking care of all the homeless people.

At last the sun came out. Work on new businesses and homes could get started. The work lasted for five years, but in time Johnstown came back to life.

Today, visitors to Johnstown do not see the terrible damage. Old newspapers are all that tell of the worst flood ever in the United States.

Think About It

1. Why was Johnstown flooded in 1889?

2. How do you think Victor Heiser felt during his wild ride in the flood?

3. Suppose Victor Heiser sent a letter to a friend, telling what happened to him. Write what he might have said about his river trip aboard a barn.

ICEMAN

by Deborah Eaton
illustrated by John A. Lytle

OF THE ALPS

On a September day in 1991, Erika and Helmut Simon were hiking in the Alps along the border between Italy and Austria. When they ventured off the path, they saw something sticking up out of the snow. It looked like a human body.

When the Simons went closer, they discovered the remains of a man frozen in the snow. They assumed it was the body of a hiker who had fallen years before.

Later, when experts told them what they had found, the Simons were astounded. This was not the body of a hiker. It was that of a man who had died there more than 5,000 years before. Frozen in the ice, his body had been preserved as a mummy. In fact, it was the oldest complete mummy ever found.

To learn how old the mummy was, experts studied the ax found with it. The blade was made of pure copper, like the blades of axes used 5,000 years ago. Carbon dating, a reliable method of finding out how old something is, was also used. It confirmed that the Iceman, as he came to be called, lived more than 5,000 years ago.

The Iceman had a fur hat and a grass
poncho, made so that rain would run off it. He wore
shoes made of hide, which he had stuffed with grass for
warmth. His pants and jacket were made from animal
skins, too. He had mended some rips in them, using a
needle made of bone and strings of grass.

In life the Iceman had been 5 feet 3 inches tall,
with blue eyes and brown hair. He had just had a
haircut—there were snips of hair in his clothing. He
was carrying a lunch of antelope meat with him.

Scouring the site where the mummy was discovered,
searchers found a variety of items belonging to the
Iceman. These objects are still being looked at by
experts whose specialty is studying artifacts.

Some of the items, so outdated to us, may have
been newfangled to the Iceman! Perhaps he made his
equipment in a sociable group around the campfire
while meat roasted on a skewer.

Items from life 5,000 years ago are scarce. We are
beginning to know more about that time now, thanks
to the Iceman.

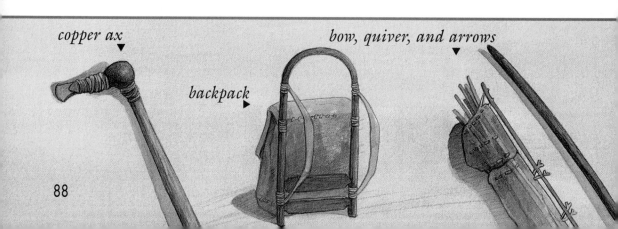

copper ax

bow, quiver, and arrows

backpack

birchbark container

stone dagger

flint

bone needle

89

The Iceman was a strong man in the prime of life, somewhere between 25 and 40 years old. How, then, did he die? There could be a variety of reasons. Maybe the animals that normally flourished nearby were scarce, and he ventured farther to hunt and got lost. Experts do know that he had a broken arm. Perhaps he broke it while experimenting with the bow he was making. Maybe, just as the Simons said at first, he fell while hiking.

Today, the rare and important mummy is preserved in a freezer. The climate inside is kept just like that of the site where the Iceman was found. Experts are still conducting experiments to study this amazing "time traveler." They believe the Iceman has more secrets to reveal about his life and time.

HOW THE ICEMAN BECAME A MUMMY

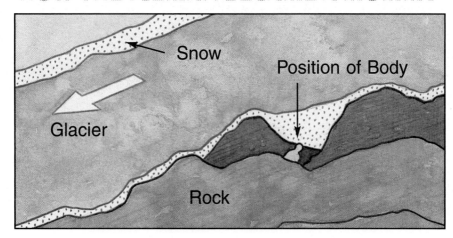

1. He fell down between two rocks.
2. Snow covered him, and he froze.
3. A glacier [GLAY•sher] formed over the two rocks.
4. After 5,000 years, the climate warmed and the ice melted.

Think About It

1. How long ago did the Iceman live? How did experts find that out?

2. Why do you think people are interested in finding out how the Iceman and others lived long ago?

3. When the Simons got home from their hiking trip, they probably told their friends what they discovered. Write what the Simons and their friends may have said.

Merry Mix-Ups

Oops! The letters of that last word are scrambled. It should be *unite*. The words *untie* and *unite* are anagrams,

Spellers of the World, Untie!

which means that you can rearrange the letters of one word to form the other. Here are some anagram sentences.

Statue of Liberty = built to stay free

the eyes = they see

the Morse code = here come dots

payment received = every cent paid me

conversation = voices rant on

the countryside = no city dust here

the detectives = detect thieves

the public art galleries = large picture halls, I bet

93

It's A Wonder!

by Susan M. Fischer

illustrated by Rick Powell

You are in a shuttle, orbiting the earth. Look down on our beautiful planet! You see the outlines of landforms. You see winding rivers and bodies of water. You see the snowy peaks of mountains.

The world's inhabitants cannot be seen from where you are. You can, however, see some evidence of civilization. Look closely. Do you see something that looks like a dragon? You are looking at one of the wonders of the world—the Great Wall of China!

The Great Wall of China is indeed a wonder. It is 4,000 miles long. That means it could stretch across the United States! It is the longest wall that has ever been made. No wonder it can be seen so far above the Earth. It is the only human-made object that can be seen from a shuttle.

The Great Wall follows the northern border of China. It runs through deserts and over hills and mountains. Of course a wall of this size wasn't made in a day. It was made over many years, by many people.

The Great Wall of China has protected China's people for more than 2,000 years. About 2,300 years ago, China's enemies were the Mongols from the north. They attacked the Chinese, damaging the terraces they had made in order to farm on their hilly land. When crops could not be grown on the terraces, famine followed. Something had to be done!

China needed a strong new leader. King Cheng became China's first emperor. His first administrative job was to protect his people from the Mongols. To do this, he had to come up with an invention that would keep enemies out. Perhaps a great wall?

The emperor knew it must be no ordinary wall. He would plan it very carefully. The Mongols were smart, but so was China's new emperor!

The great wall must be both tall and strong to keep enemies out. It must have watchtowers with lookout posts. Its top must serve as a road, which should be wide enough for ten people or five horses. The wall King Cheng planned would indeed be a great wall.

Before long, the emperor's elaborate plan was underway. He ordered thousands of men to work on the Great Wall. Some made bricks from clay. Some pounded the earth into tall mounds. Some cut stone. The work was long and hard.

Many of the workers did not live to see the wall completed. Overwork killed them, and the wall became their tomb. Yet that tomb saved the lives of countless thousands more by protecting them from the danger of attack.

The wall was slowly taking shape. Towers were made to watch for Mongols. When the wall was finished, they would no longer get in to kill and rob and damage.

An army of 300,000 people labored 14 years to finish the wall. When it was finally completed, it looked like an immense snake. It twisted and turned over terraces and mountains.

An old Chinese tale claims that the Great Wall is a dragon that turned to stone. The "dragon" stands always ready to protect China from its enemies, just as the emperor planned.

Today the world sees China as a great power. Of all the inhabitants of the earth, one in five lives in China.

The Chinese civilization is one of the oldest in the world. It has always been known for its clever inventions, and the Great Wall is evidence of its inventive power. No wonder it's a wonder to people around the world—and above it!

Think About It

1. How long and how wide is the Great Wall of China? Why is it so big?

2. How do you think the people who constructed the Great Wall of China felt about the project? Why do you think that?

3. You visit the Great Wall of China and go up to walk along it. Then you write a postcard about it to a friend at home. Write what you tell your friend.

Treasures of the Pharaoh

by Doris Licameli
illustrated by Adair Payne

In the Valley of the Kings, near Cairo, Egypt, the tombs of the pharaohs lie hidden under the sand. With ingenious planning to prevent robbery, the tombs were cut into the rocky hillsides long, long ago. In time, they were forgotten and lost.

In 1922, a man named Howard Carter returned to Egypt. His job was to study the artifacts of early Egypt. Carter had been to Egypt many times to search for lost tombs, but this trip was very important. Lord Carnarvon, his sponsor, had told him this was the last search he would pay for.

Giza

Cairo

The Valley of the Kings

Nile River

The famous pyramids of Egypt were built using stone from quarries along the Nile. After these were robbed, pharaohs built their tombs in the cliffs of the Valley of Kings.

Howard Carter and his helpers found hidden steps under the desert sand in 1922.

On their first day of exploring, Carter and his workers made a lucky find. They stumbled upon a hidden flight of steps!

The workers excavated sixteen steps, which led down to a doorway deep inside the hill. Could this be a pharaoh's tomb?

Carter tried to control his rising optimism. He knew that other tombs at this isolated site had been found vacant. Grave robbers had stripped them bare long ago, just as they had stripped the chambers of the pyramids.

There were royal seals around the doorway. A good sign! The opening was blocked with stones that were plastered over. The plaster showed signs that it had been broken through and repaired. Carter could only hope for the best.

When the stones had been removed, Carter could see a passageway that had been blocked up with stones. He was delighted! Here was evidence that there might be something inside that needed to be protected.

The suspense grows as Carter discovers vacant space beyond the sealed doorway.

After the workers excavated the passageway, Carter found a second doorway just like the first. It, too, showed signs that the tomb had been opened and closed before.

Carter made a tiny hole in this doorway and put a test rod into it. The rod went through, showing there must be a chamber of some kind on the other side!

Carter's tension grew. It might be only a false passageway, like some in the pyramids. Carter called for candles to check whether the air on the other side had harmful gases in it.

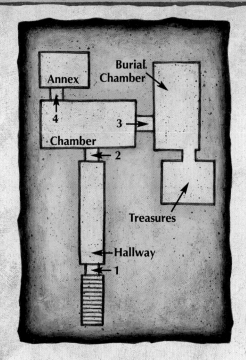

King Tut's tomb was planned so as to protect it from robbers.

Burial Chamber

Annex

Chamber

Treasures

Hallway

1–First Doorway
2–Second Doorway
3–Third Doorway
4–Fourth Doorway

Holding a candle to the peephole he had made, Carter got his first glimpse of the chamber beyond. The stunning sight delighted him. Piles of gold treasures glowed in the light of the flame! He saw a gold throne, a king's robes, baskets of preserved food, and even beds shaped like animals. The people of Egypt believed in an afterlife and had given their king everything he would need.

Carter learned that the tomb he had discovered was the long-lost tomb of Tutankhamun, called King Tut for short by historians and archaeologists. Tut had taken the throne when he was only nine years old and died when he was eighteen.

Tut's burial chambers gleamed with gold. The young king's preserved body lay in a set of three gold coffins. The face of the mummy was covered by a mask of solid gold.

More than 3,000 objects were found in Tut's tomb. It took Carter and his helpers more than ten years to list them all.

Today, visitors to the Cairo Museum in Egypt can see most of the treasures of Tutankhamun. Many people in the United States have seen some of them in a traveling display. But no one will ever see them quite as Howard Carter first did, in a dark tomb by candlelight.

King Tut's burial mask is made of solid gold. It weighs 22.5 pounds.

Think About It

1. What did Howard Carter find in the sands of Egypt?

2. Why do you think King Tut's treasures were still in his burial chamber, even though the robbers had emptied the tombs of most other pharaohs?

3. On the day Carter found King Tut's tomb, he probably described his find in his journal. Write Carter's journal entry for that day.

Archaeo-Jokes

You probably know that -*ology* means "the study of."
The Greek word part *archaeo-* indicates "ancient,"
so *archaeology* means "the study of ancient times."

Where was the archaeologist when the lights went out?
    In the dark.

What note did the musician sing as she viewed
the sights from the top of a pyramid?
    High see.

How would you describe a pyramid with no top?
    Pointless.

What kind of music did the pyramid builders like best?
    Rock.

What did the archaeologist
name her son?
    Doug.

Can you come out to play?

I don't know. I'll have to ask my mummy.

VESUVIUS: A.D. 79

by John Reed

This wall painting shows Mount Vesuvius in Roman times. The volcano had only one cone, and trees grew to the top.

IT WAS A LITTLE BEFORE ONE O'CLOCK on a summer day in the ancient city of Pompeii. The year was A.D. 79.

Most people were getting ready for lunch. At the bakery, loaves of bread browned in the ovens. At the market in the city center, shoppers picked up fresh figs.

The people of Pompeii had no idea that the mountain was dangerous. Here they follow their familiar routines.

Suddenly, there was a terrible roar. The sky turned black, and lightning sliced the air, but this was no thunderstorm. Rocks, ash, and cinders clattered onto houses and bounced onto streets.

Pompeii was situated at the base of Mount Vesuvius. Everyone knew that Vesuvius was a volcano, but for 300 years, it had been quiet. Then, on that sunny day, the mountain exploded.

In a few hours Pompeii was almost covered with rock and ash. Only the tops of the houses showed.

Later, when the volcano became quiet once again, people tried to dig out parts of the city. They found the job too big, however, and had to give up. It was more important to find new homes for the citizens who had escaped.

Over hundreds of years, layers of earth covered everything. Not a trace of the city could be seen. People, animals, houses, shops, and theaters all lay in silence under the thick volcanic ash. In time, Pompeii was forgotten.

Shops like these were soon deep in ash and cinders.

Wall paintings show scenes of daily life.

ONE DAY IN 1594, some workers were digging a tunnel when their shovels hit a wall. They decided to brush away the dirt and take a closer look. The wall had pictures painted on it. "How interesting," they said. Then they went back to work on the tunnel.

Amazingly, more than 150 years went by before someone figured out why that wall was there. A man named Alcubierre knew that long before, cities in this ancient Roman province had been covered when a volcano erupted. He believed that this wall was part of one of those cities.

Many of Pompeii's citizens attended plays and musical performances.

In 1763, Alcubierre and 24 diggers set to work. They were the first of many, many people to take part in excavating Pompeii. Artifacts from the site have helped people reconstruct what daily life was like in the ancient Roman Empire.

Because it covered everything, the volcanic ash formed a time capsule of Pompeii at the time of the disaster. That's how we know bread was baking in the bakery's oven at the moment when Vesuvius erupted. The loaves, like an emblem of everyday life, were still there when the cinders were cleared away. The figs, in their glass containers, were still in the marketplace.

The ancient city's architecture tells us much about the people who lived there. The two theaters show that Pompeii's citizens attended plays. The large public baths show that the people had high standards for hygiene. Many of the walls around the city have paintings on them. These pictures add to the story.

Water for the public baths came from wells. Later, aqueducts were used to carry water long distances.

Much of Pompeii has now been uncovered. People can once again walk its streets and see its artifacts and architecture, mosaics and wall paintings.

In many ways, Pompeii is just like a modern city. Houses of all sizes are situated near stores, lunch counters, and barber shops. Each place tells a story about a lively city that met with disaster on a long-ago summer day.

Many of Pompeii's stories have yet to be uncovered.

Think About It

1. What happened to the city of Pompeii in A.D. 79? Why did people forget about Pompeii?

2. Why do you think people are still excavating Pompeii?

3. Suppose that you lived not far from Pompeii in A.D. 79. You were safe, but you could see what was happening. Describe what you saw.

The Wisdom *of* Jefferson

by Meish Goldish
illustrated by Robert Nubecker

CHARACTERS

NARRATOR
RICHARD HENRY LEE
JOHN DICKINSON
JOHN ADAMS
BENJAMIN FRANKLIN
THOMAS JEFFERSON

SCENE 1

TIME: *June, 1776*
SETTING: *Independence Hall, Philadelphia*

NARRATOR: Welcome to the Second Continental Congress! Step inside—you're just in time for the debate on the topic of American independence. Let's hear what the members of Congress are saying.

RICHARD HENRY LEE: Gentlemen, it's time we declared ourselves independent of England! The American colonies must be free from King George!

JOHN DICKINSON: Oh, stop your bellowing, Mr. Lee! Who are you to judge King George? I believe we can work out our disagreements with him.

JOHN ADAMS: No, Mr. Dickinson! Those in England who rule us do us no honor. They place huge taxes on us but grant us no rights! They are rigid and stingy brutes!

JOHN DICKINSON: Are your virtues any better, Mr. Adams?

BENJAMIN FRANKLIN: Gentlemen! Please stop all this and stick to the topic. Perhaps we need to write a document that explains why our country must be free.

JOHN DICKINSON: And who will write such a document?

BENJAMIN FRANKLIN: We are most fortunate to have in this Congress one who has excellent writing skills. He also has the energy of an athlete and wisdom beyond his youth. I call upon Thomas Jefferson to write us a document that will make clear our case.

THOMAS JEFFERSON: I'll do it!

SCENE 2

TIME: *Two weeks later*
SETTING: *Same*

THOMAS JEFFERSON (*dramatically finishing his reading of the Declaration of Independence to Congress*): ". . . we . . . pledge to each other our lives, our fortunes, and our sacred honor."

JOHN ADAMS (*taking the scroll from Jefferson and holding it up*): What a gem! This Declaration will rouse King George and force him to grant us independence!

JOHN DICKINSON: It may just make things worse.

THOMAS JEFFERSON: We're already at war with him. How can things get worse? The Declaration of Independence will let the British know that we mean business!

JOHN DICKINSON: Yes, Mr. Jefferson, but England's army is five times as large as ours! Your Declaration won't scare it away!

THOMAS JEFFERSON: Mr. Dickinson, just what is it about independence that you find so terrible?

JOHN DICKINSON: No colony has ever broken away from its parent country. We have no right to do it.

THOMAS JEFFERSON: We have every right! All people have the right to life, liberty, and happiness.

JOHN DICKINSON: Not everyone agrees with your Declaration, Mr. Jefferson. I, for one, think it a dangerous document disguised as a democratic one. In my judgment, it will do more damage than good.

BENJAMIN FRANKLIN: How can it do that? We are already an independent country, living apart from England. We might as well declare it. I think the members of Congress will vote in favor of Jefferson's Declaration.

JOHN DICKINSON: We shall see, sir.

SCENE 3

TIME: *July 4, 1776*
SETTING: *Same*

RICHARD HENRY LEE: Well done, Jefferson! The Declaration of Independence passed the vote!

JOHN ADAMS: We are free from England! How fortunate I feel!

BENJAMIN FRANKLIN: How do you feel, Thomas?

THOMAS JEFFERSON *(holding his scroll)*: Most honored, sir. I feel like an athlete who has just won a long race!

NARRATOR: The wisdom of Jefferson's Declaration of Independence guided the new country in its youth. Today we still rely on Jefferson's wisdom to help us keep our country strong.

Think About It

1. Why did John Dickinson worry about the Declaration Thomas Jefferson had written?

2. Why do you think Jefferson said he felt like an athlete who had just won a long race?

3. What do you think the King of England and his advisors said when they first read the Declaration of Independence? Write your ideas in the form of a short play.

Follow the

"We're lost, Joy! I just know we're lost!" I could feel the first stirrings of panic deep inside.

"Stop fretting, Danny!" my cousin snapped, annoyed with my whining. Then her voice changed. "Don't worry—it's not that big a deal. We'll find our way back to Uncle Leroy's, or he'll find us."

Wild Geese

by Ron Gellar illustrated by Jeffrey Lindberg

We were seated on sun-warmed boulders, feet dangling, in a remote clearing surrounded by dense forest. Exploring our uncle's new property, we had somehow gotten turned around. Now we didn't know how to reverse our steps to get back.

Uncle Leroy's property was on the south shore of a bay on the beautiful blue Pacific. It was a crisp October day, and most of the leaves had changed to their bright fall colors. Joy and I, visiting, had decided to take a walk to the nearby forest and collect some. First we had followed the rocky shore past an old lighthouse with a cracked foundation. Then we had turned off into the forest onto a road made of crushed oyster shells.

Delighted with the glowing fall colors all around us, we'd wandered for some time beneath the trees. We had fun shuffling through the fallen leaves and showering each other with golden armfuls of them. Heads bent low, we gathered the very finest specimens to take home in our backpacks. When we looked up again, ready to go, the oyster-shell road was nowhere to be seen. Search as we might, we couldn't find our way back to it. We were lost.

"I'm so hungry," I complained.

Joy presented me with a handful of slightly squashed berries from her backpack. "I didn't pick these here," she said, seeing my wary look, "so they won't poison you. They're from Uncle Leroy's berry patch, and they're perfectly edible."

I frowned at the shriveled berries. "I need something more nourishing than those. Too bad pizza doesn't grow on bushes. I'm starving!"

Joy munched and swallowed. "Try some, Danny. They're not bad—better than nothing, at least. It's lucky I picked them."

What choice did I have? I took some and popped them in my mouth. They tasted like blackberries and left purple stains on my hands, which I wiped on my corduroy pants. Luckily the pants were dark, so a little purple wouldn't show when we got home. IF we got home.

A squirrel stuck its head out of a dark cavity in a tree. Maybe it had stored nuts in there that we could eat. I jumped down from my boulder and hurried into the dense thicket, but it was impossible to find the right tree. I did, however, find a shallow creek with tiny, darting fish.

"Joy, come here," I yelled. I stretched out on the moist soil of the bank and dangled my fingers in the water. Joy joined me, and we drank the ice-cold creek water from our cupped hands.

"If only we could catch some of these fish!" I said.

"They're much too quick for us," Joy pointed out. "Besides, I don't know how to clean fish, and we have no way to fry them."

"No, and I wouldn't want to just gulp them down, would you?" I grinned at her, and she made a face.

"Yuck!" we both said together.

It was getting late in the day, and the setting sun began to cast long shadows. Deep shade filled our clearing, and our boulders were no longer warm to sit on.

I pulled my sweater closer against the chill in the air. Joy sighed. "We may have to spend the night here," she said.

This discouraging piece of news made me sigh, too. It would be freezing out here when it got really dark. I wondered whether piles of leaves would be enough to keep us warm.

Just at that point I heard a remote honking noise. As the sound came closer, we saw flocks of wild geese flying high above us. Pointing upward, I said, "Isn't it neat the way they fly in a V?"

"It's migration time," Joy said. "They're going south for the winter." Then she stopped and looked at me. "Danny! Uncle Leroy's place is on the south side of the bay!"

"Of course!" I exclaimed. "All we need to do is follow the wild geese! We're not lost after all!"

It was just that simple. We followed the geese south until we found ourselves back at the oyster-shell road. The road led us out of the forest to the sparkling bay, a most welcome sight. Following its rocky shore southward, we cheered as we passed the old lighthouse with the cracked foundation. Not far beyond it, we knew, lay Uncle Leroy's house.

The wild geese still had a long way to fly to their winter feeding grounds. But we were home in time for dinner.

Think About It

1. How do Joy and Danny get lost? How do they get back to Uncle Leroy's house?

2. How do you think Joy and Danny feel about the wild geese? Why do you think that?

3. At the end of the day, both Joy and Danny write in their diaries. They describe what happened and discuss their feelings. Choose one of the main characters and write his or her diary entry.

Daffynitions

geese: an oil, as in "You need to put some geese on that lock so it'll open."

macaw: vehicle belonging to me, as in "Macaw wouldn't start this morning."

hawk: to sound a horn, as in "Hawk your horn to warn folks you're coming."

sparrow: to part with, as in "Can you sparrow few coins for a phone call?"

starling: a tiny star

myna: a person who digs coal out of the ground

133

MUSIC IN THE AIR

by Pam Zollman

illustrated by Rian Hughes

"I can't do it," I cried in despair, resting my hands on the piano keys.

"Shake your fingers, Audrey," Mom said, "and try again."

"What's the point? I know I'll never be ready in time for the recital," I said. To my mind, my playing sounded awful. It was getting worse, not better. I couldn't seem to play my piece once through without a flaw.

My brother, Paul, quipped, "I'll let the newspaper know that the star performer isn't ready yet."

Paul's comment annoyed me because I've never seen myself as a star. To tell the truth, I don't think I'm very good on the piano.

The rest of my family members have various musical talents that bring them applause. Grandma sings, Dad plays the violin, Paul plays the drums, and Mom plays the piano. I think my family's musical legacy has stopped with me.

Ignoring Paul, Mom said, "Maybe you've practiced too much, Audrey. You've been playing all morning. Why don't you take a rest, and we'll go for a walk."

Mom packed a wicker picnic basket with some sandwiches and lemonade. We walked down a slope to a field of wildflowers not far from our home.

We laid a blanket on the grass and sat. All around us birds chirped, squirrels chattered, and insects buzzed. Above us, the beautiful song of a mockingbird drifted on the breeze. Their cheerful sounds were so melodious.

"Do you hear that, Audrey?" Mom asked, smiling at me. "Music is in the air."

"Too bad it's not in me," I quipped.

"It is," Mom said, "but you must reach deep inside yourself to feel the music."

"I don't seem to know how," I said. "Help me, Mom."

"Think of it this way," Mom said. "There's a concert being performed all the time, but you must listen carefully in order to hear it."

I sat still and soaked up the lilting presentation of the music-makers around me.

"The piano was hard for me, too, at first," Mom confessed, "but I persevered. Once I found the music inside me, I began to have success."

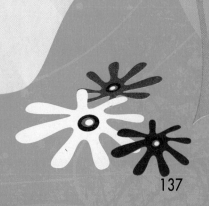

After our picnic, we took a different way home. Cars in a hurry and trucks hauling loads rushed by us.

"What do you hear?" asked Mom.

"Noisy traffic," I said. "A confusing commotion."

Mom caught my hand. "Listen closely. Music is in the air! The various squealing brakes, roaring engines, loud mufflers, honking horns, and wailing sirens all blend together. Each one adds to the pulsing beat."

It wasn't the sweetest music, but Mom was right. She had taught me to hear street music.

That night, as I lay in bed, I heard new harmonies. The yelping and howling of a nearby dog blended with the distant wail of a train. The deep croaking of a bullfrog contrasted with the light chirping of crickets. Night music, I saw, was melodious in its own way.

I was still worried about performing at the recital, but I was beginning to feel the music inside me.

The morning of the recital, Paul said, "Audrey, just have pride in yourself and you'll do fine tonight. After all, you passed your audition to get into City Music School. That shows you have talent—they take only the best."

That evening, when I sat down at the piano on the theater stage, I paused for a moment. As the audience awaited my performance, I remembered the field concert, the street music, and the night music. I remembered my audition and how much I've learned since then. I might not be a flawless performer, but I knew now that the music was in me.

I began to play, newly confident, and music filled the air.

Think About It

1. How does Audrey's mom help her get ready for the recital?

2. Do you think Audrey really lacks the musical talent that the other members of her family have? Explain.

3. After the recital, Audrey and her mom go for another walk. What might they talk about this time? Write the conversation they have.

Invented by Mistake

by William Bailey   **illustrated by David Diaz**

Think of all the things we use in our everyday lives. Some of them are very practical, making our lives safer and easier. For example, windshield wipers were invented to improve visibility in bad weather. Others simply make our lives more fun. Now think of how these things got started. Have we always had them? Of course not! Someone had to invent them.

Many inventions take years to develop. Inventors have acknowledged that it could take persistence and ingenuity to work out the details. Other inventions, however, are the result of pure luck.

Here are the stories behind several such lucky inventions. The amazing thing about these inventions is that they were invented by mistake!

RAISINS Have you ever tried eating a dried grape? Of course you have! Dried grapes are better known as raisins. The first raisins came from the western United States, where many farmers grow grapes. At that time, most grapes were sold to be eaten fresh.

In 1873, a severe heat wave struck the grape-growing valleys. The grapes shriveled and dried up. Things looked bad for the growers.

One practical farmer simply refused to lose the whole crop. He tasted some of the shriveled grapes and discovered they were good. The farmer took the dried grapes to a local store. There he showed how they could be used for snacking and baking. People loved them! Soon other stores were making inquiries about this new food. We've eaten raisins ever since.

143

MAPLE SYRUP A Native American legend says that maple syrup was discovered by an Indian chief and his wife. One spring, the chief left his ax stuck in the trunk of a tree overnight. By morning, sap had dripped into a pail beneath that tree, which happened to be a maple.

The chief and his wife took home the pail of "tree water." Later that day, the wife decided she would use this water to cook their supper in. As the sap boiled, it became thick and sweet. When the chief tasted his supper that night, he was thrilled. He was enjoying the world's first maple syrup!

COLA DRINKS In 1886, a man had a headache and wanted to mix up a remedy for it. He began cooking some different ingredients together in a big kettle. One of the things he added was a bunch of cola nuts. He smiled when he drank the finished product. It tasted so good that he forgot all about his headache.

Later he added water to the mix and poured it over ice. It was even better that way! Then one day, by mistake, he added bubbly soda water rather than plain water. This version of the drink was a real treat! He knew he had made something other people would want. He had not met his initial goal of finding a headache remedy. He had invented something better—the first cola drink!

145

CHOCOLATE CHIP COOKIES A baker's mistake became a milestone in the history of cookies. In 1930, Ruth Wakefield was making chocolate cookies for the people staying at the Toll House Inn. As she was mixing the batter, she realized she had forgotten to get baker's chocolate. When she saw a bar of dark chocolate on the shelf, she had an inspiration. She broke up the bar and added the bits to the batter. She hoped the bits would melt, making chocolate cookies.

When Ruth took the cookies out of the oven, she got a surprise. The chocolate hadn't melted but had stayed in little chunks. This new version of the chocolate cookie became very popular.

ICE-CREAM CONES When you order ice cream, you probably get it in a cone. It hasn't always been sold this way, however.

On a hot afternoon at the 1904 World's Fair, an ice cream vendor ran out of dishes. The quick-thinking vendor, noticing that thin, crispy waffles were being sold nearby, had an inspiration. He simply purchased a stack of the waffles and rolled each one into a cone. Then he scooped the ice cream into the cones and went right on serving his customers.

Waffle cones became very popular. Soon another man, F. Bruckman, invented a way to manufacture them. Now the ice cream cone is one of the most popular ways to enjoy ice cream.

Think About It

1. Name four things that were invented by mistake.

2. How do you think Ruth Wakefield felt when she took her cookies out of the oven? How do you think her feelings changed?

3. Think of another item you use in your everyday life. How might that item have been invented by mistake? Write your own story of that invention.

Cook's Comedy

First Comedian: I went to a French restaurant, and they had snails on the menu.

Second Comedian: I would never eat snails.

First Comedian: Why not?

Second Comedian: Because I prefer fast food.

Diner in a Restaurant: Do you serve crabs?

Waiter: Yes, sir. We serve everybody.

Pizza Server: Would you like your pizza cut into six slices or eight?

Customer: Six. I don't think I'm hungry enough to eat eight slices.

Cheddar: Care to join me in a pizza?

Mozzarella: That would be just grate!

First Comedian: I served something yesterday that I wouldn't want to eat.

Second Comedian: What was that?

First Comedian: A tennis ball.

149

Honorable Mention

by Edward Cruz
illustrated by Jesse Reisch

Rudy and Brent cruised through the middle school crowd and started for home.

"Your basset hound painting is going to win the Dog Show Art Contest," Rudy said.

Brent held up his hand, imitating a traffic officer. "Whoa! I don't know about that. *Your* drawing of a bulldog is super realistic. Well, the judges will decide, but our little rivalry is dependent on your finishing by Tuesday."

Rudy held out his drawing and examined it closely. "It still needs a lot of work before it's ready to put on display," he declared.

After Brent turned the corner to his place, Rudy noticed a small dog trotting briskly beside him. He stooped down to pet the pup. Then he waved his arms. "Go home now," he said firmly, but the determined stray remained underfoot. Rudy tried to outrun him, but the frisky pooch tagged along with him all the way home. When Rudy opened the front door of his apartment, the pup squeezed in and followed him to his bedroom.

Rudy put his backpack and drawing on his bed and squatted down to rub the dog's velvety ears. "I bet your family is looking for you. You're a natural pet, aren't you?" The dog yipped as if to agree and licked Rudy's chin.

Rudy called Brent, who came over and admired the pup. "How will you find the owner, Rudy?" he asked.

"Since he doesn't have a collar and tags, I'm going to make a drawing of him to post around town. That way the owner can call us," Rudy said. He took out his sketching materials and, with confident, delicate strokes, began drawing.

"He looks as if he might be a miniature collie," said Brent.

Rudy nodded. "I think he's a Shetland sheepdog." He drew the dog's natural markings, which looked like boots, a cape, and a mask.

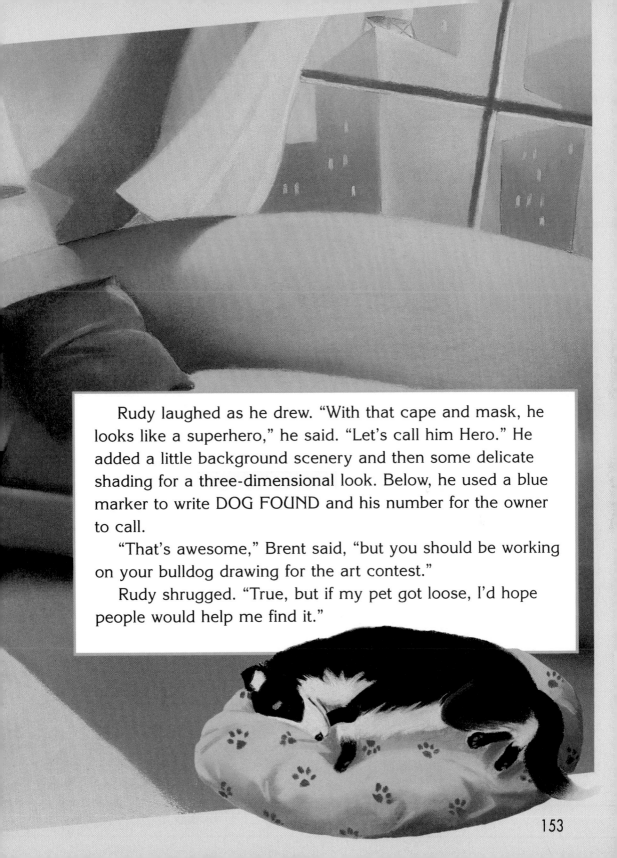

Rudy laughed as he drew. "With that cape and mask, he looks like a superhero," he said. "Let's call him Hero." He added a little background scenery and then some delicate shading for a three-dimensional look. Below, he used a blue marker to write DOG FOUND and his number for the owner to call.

"That's awesome," Brent said, "but you should be working on your bulldog drawing for the art contest."

Rudy shrugged. "True, but if my pet got loose, I'd hope people would help me find it."

"Okay, let's take your drawing to the copy shop," said Brent. "I'll help you pay." The boys gave Hero a plate of scraps and a bowl of water and shut him in Rudy's room. Soon they were tacking up his portrait around town.

When Rudy got home and opened the door to his room, Hero was glad to see him. The dog trotted proudly to a pile of chewed paper—Rudy's bulldog drawing!

"Oh, no!" Rudy groaned. He sagged to the floor, staring at the chewed bits. Then he called Brent. "Sorry, but I'm out of the contest," he said sadly. As he explained what had happened, he stroked the dog curled up beside him. He knew there was no valid reason to blame the pup. It was his own fault for leaving the drawing lying about.

On Friday night, the dog's owner called. After speaking to Rudy's mom, he agreed to come by their apartment on Saturday to pick him up. Rudy and Brent played catch with Hero until his owner came. When it was time to say good-bye, Rudy gave the pooch a quick hug. Hero had chewed up his artwork, but he still liked him.

"Thank you for your effort to return my dog," the owner said. He shook Rudy's hand. "I'd like to mention that it was an honorable thing to do."

He jingled his dog's collar. "If that rascal hadn't slipped out of this, you could have simply called me. I'm amazed at how perfectly you represented his markings in your drawing. My first reaction was that it was the work of a natural artist."

Rudy enjoyed the compliment and felt good about helping.

Rudy's smile drooped a little on Tuesday when he and Brent went to the art contest. He couldn't help wishing that he had a drawing entered, too. Brent's basset hound painting hung on display with a blue ribbon. "You deserve it, pal," Rudy said. "We may use different materials, but we're both good artists."

"That's true," said Brent, pointing to another drawing with an Honorable Mention ribbon on it. He chuckled at Rudy's confused reaction. "You left the original of your drawing of Hero at my place. I just cut off the words and entered it. Our art teacher said it would be a perfectly valid entry."

Rudy grinned. "That makes two Honorable Mentions—first from the dog owner and then from the contest! Thanks, Brent."

Brent grinned back. "I'd say that kind of recognition equals a blue ribbon! Let's declare a tie."

The two artists shook on that.

Think About It

1. How does Rudy help Hero and his owner?

2. How does Rudy feel when Hero's owner comes to get him?

3. The local newspaper prints a story about the Dog Show Art Contest. Write the news story that appears in the paper.

157

Making Freedom's Bell

by Lee Chang

illustrated by Charles Passarelli

More than 250 years ago, metalworker John Stow fired up his furnace for an important piece of work. He had been asked to make the bell for the tower of the Pennsylvania State House. He had no idea that the bell he was about to cast would become a symbol of freedom for a new country.

In 1752 a bell for the State House had been made at Whitechapel Foundry in London. However, a 2,080 pound bell is not really portable. It was probably damaged during its long voyage. When the bell arrived in Philadelphia, it was unloaded, unwrapped, and tested. To everyone's horror, when the clapper knocked against it, the bell cracked!

Pennsylvania's leaders were not willing to install a cracked bell. They decided to ask John Stow to make a new one. Stow had a knack for working with metal. He hoped one day to modernize his foundry. Meanwhile, working at his forge, he made everything from ornamental candlesticks to ordinary tools. The only bells he had cast, however, were horse bells.

John Stow was honored to be assigned this job. He knew he would need help with such a large, important project. Not much is known about the assistant he chose. John Pass may have been a skilled artist or simply an apprentice.

Stow and Pass made clay molds of both the outside and inside of the bell. The space between the two would be the mold for the new bell. The mouth of the bell had to be perfectly round, not oval.

Then, using sledgehammers, the two strong, rugged men broke up the original bell. They melted the scraps, and Stow made the decision to add more copper for extra strength. They poured the molten metal into the mold, and by April 1753 the bell was ready. Larger than anything John Stow had ever made before, the bell was as beautiful as a sculpture.

Everyone was eager to hear the bell's first clear bong-g-g. To John Stow's dismay, the bell made an ugly clank like the sound of two shovels being knocked together. Stow's profit no longer mattered to him. He just wanted his "sculpture" to sound as beautiful as it looked.

The problem gnawed at Stow. What had gone wrong? Had the bell's mouth turned out slightly oval? Once again, Stow and Pass broke up the bell. Stow decided to use less copper. The two men may have received help from other apprentices this time because it took them only two months to finish.

When the third bell was hung up for a test, John Stow held his breath and his knees trembled. If this bell was a success, perhaps he would finally earn enough money to modernize his shop. It was not just a matter of profit, however. It was a matter of pride.

Bong-g-g-g! Bong-g-g-g! The sound was loud and clear. A cheer rose from the crowd, and applause filled the air. Stow smiled, proud and relieved.

The bell was raised to the tower of the State House. Philadelphia held a huge feast in honor of Stow and Pass. People paid many tributes to the two ordinary workers who had created an extraordinary bell.

Pennsylvania's leaders were very pleased. Stow and Pass's large bell could be heard from farther away than any bell they'd had. The leaders would be able to use the bell to call people to meetings.

No one knew that 23 years later, the bell would be rung at the first reading of the Declaration of Independence. No one knew it would one day become a national symbol called the Liberty Bell. In 1753 it was just the State House bell.

Unfortunately John Stow never made another bell. He died the next year. There is no further record of John Pass. However, the two bell makers will never be forgotten. Written in large letters on the Liberty Bell are the words *Pass and Stow*.

Think About It

1. Why was a new bell made for the Pennsylvania State House?

2. How do you think John Stow would have felt if he had known the third bell would become the Liberty Bell?

3. John Stow might have written in his journal to record his feelings on the day he and John Pass tested the third bell. Write a journal entry Stow could have written.

A Summer Treat

by Marco Antunez

Illustrated by Richard Stergul

I was staring into space, my mind focused on the girl who had just moved in up the street. Suddenly I became aware that my father was staring, too—at me.

"Mike, are you daydreaming again?"

"Yes, Dad," I said a little sheepishly.

"Well, I hate to interrupt," he said jokingly, "but could I ask you to do me a favor?"

"Sure," I said. "What do you need?"

Dad held up a small bag. "I need you to deliver this medicine to Mrs. Farber," he said. "Her three little ones are all sick. Can you find this address?" He looked at me uncertainly. He knew my mind was on other things.

"Oh, I'm sure I can find Grant Avenue," I said with conviction. Dad really likes it when I figure things out for myself.

"Okay," he said. "Get it there as fast as you can. Mrs. Farber is waiting for it, and I told her I'd rush it to her."

Outside, I scowled as I jumped on my bike. It was an awfully hot day, so I hoped this errand wouldn't take too long.

Shoppers were bustling up and down Main Street. I could ask one of them how to get to Grant Avenue. With any luck, I'd find it easily and be back inside sipping an icy cold drink before I knew it.

The man I asked said Grant Avenue was across town near the library. That wouldn't be too confusing because I go to the library all the time.

I smiled and hummed as I propelled myself toward Grant Avenue. Dad's always telling me to figure things out for myself. Well, this time I'd done just that!

Number 257 Grant Avenue was situated in the middle of the block. Dropping my bike, I leaped up the steps, carefully avoiding the scattered toys. When I rang the door bell, I had no idea of the surprise that awaited me.

The door was opened by the girl who had moved in on our street! This was very confusing. "What are you doing here?" I said, staring at her.

"What do you mean?" she asked.

"Uh—nothing," I said, anxious to avoid making a fool of myself. "This is for Mrs. Farber."

"Thanks," she said. She reviewed the label and paid me but made no move to leave the doorway.

I stood there, too, but I didn't know what to say.

"Anything else?" she asked.

"Didn't you just move to Main Street?" I finally blurted out.

"Yes," she said, "but I'm helping my mom's friend while her kids aren't feeling well. I'm Sally Gomez, by the way."

"I'm Mike Graph," I said. "I live just down the street from you, over Graph's pharmacy. What grade will you be in?"

"Grade seven," she replied.

"Me too!" I said. "Maybe we'll be in some of the same classes. I'm taking photography for an elective. Do you know what classes you're taking?"

"I'm taking photography, too," she said. "Maybe you can tell me about the campus some time."

"Some time" turned out to be later that afternoon. We met at the library, and I told Sally all about the campus. I even offered to show her around on the first day. We laughed and had a great time. Later, when I reviewed the day, I realized how lucky I was to have met her. I couldn't wait for school to start up again!

Today I'm on my way to Grant Avenue again with more medicine for Mrs. Farber's kids. Until they're well and Sally's free, at least I have a reason to visit her.

Dad seemed a little anxious when I left. "Don't take all day!" he said, glancing at his watch.

Then he winked.

Think About It

1. How does Mike meet the girl who has just moved to Main Street?

2. How do you think Sally feels about meeting Mike? What makes you think that?

3. On the day she meets Mike Graph, Sally Gomez sends an e-mail to a friend in her old hometown. Write the message Sally sends her friend.

Define It!

A pharmacy gets its name from *pharmakon*, which is a Greek word for "medicine."

not a real physician	mock doc
plenty of cotton	enough fluff
one-and-only calling instrument	lone phone
where health workers keep money	nurses' purses
didn't get an injection	not shot
joke that cracks up all the hospital workers	staff laugh

173

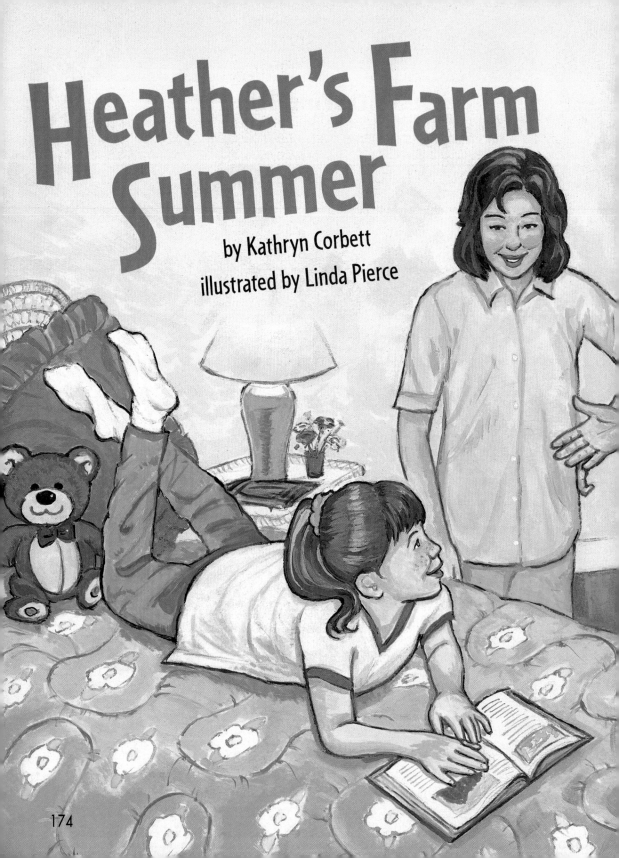

Heather's Farm Summer

by Kathryn Corbett

illustrated by Linda Pierce

Just before sixth grade began, I was adopted into a wonderful family. My new grandparents visited at each holiday. However, I did not get out to their farm during the school year.

As summer approached, we had some bad news. Grandpa had been taken ill and would be in the hospital for some time. Mom and Dad made tentative plans for helping Grandma out.

"Heather," Dad said to me, "summer is a time of heavy work on a farm. Mom and I can't leave our jobs, but would you be willing to spend the summer on the farm helping Grandma?"

Mom explained, "Even when Grandpa comes home, he won't be able to work."

I looked from one kind face to the other, feeling anxious. I had always been a city girl and knew nothing about farms, so I was hesitant. Would I be able to contribute anything useful?

I had been looking forward to a pleasant summer in the city. I planned to enjoy late, lazy breakfasts and to read outdoors in the warm weather—it was going to be heaven! Something told me farm life would not be so relaxed. Yet my new family meant so much to me, and I readily understood the problem.

I took a deep breath, mustered a smile, and said, "I'll do it!" Mom and Dad smiled back appreciatively.

The day after school ended, we drove out to the farm. It was on a huge spread of land. Excited, I leapt from the car as soon as Dad had parked.

"What a relief that you're here!" Grandma cried, hugging me. Dad quietly gestured that he would go ahead of us with my heavy bags. He and Mom stayed for lunch and then headed back to the city.

"Well, Heather," Grandma said, "now that you're settled in, are you ready for farm life?"

"I am, Grandma," I said. "Just show me how I can contribute."

"You can start by baking some bread," Grandma said, handing me the flour canister.

"Bake bread?" I was mystified. Bread was something you depended on stores for, wasn't it?

"We're far from a grocery store here, so I bake my own," Grandma explained.

Baking turned out to be fun, and the fresh bread tasted heavenly! We chatted as we snacked on it.

Grandma said, "Grandpa has always done the heavy work for me, so I dreaded this summer because of my inability to do it. Now, with a healthy helper like you, it's no longer such a concern."

Grandma's words had significance for me. They indicated that I had a way to contribute to this fine family.

Next morning, I awoke at the rooster's crow, jumped out of bed, and got ready for the day's work.

"What's for breakfast?" I asked.

"Eggs from the chickens and milk from the cows," Grandma said, smiling.

In the henhouse, I learned the signs that indicate a hen has laid an egg. When we moved on to the barn, I confessed my inability to milk cows.

"Don't feel threatened by their size," Grandma said. "They're gentle, and I'll show you what to do."

Before many days passed, I could do every chore on the farm. I was proud that Grandma depended on me, which also made me more confident.

Grandpa soon came home from the hospital, and spent his days relaxing on the porch. It was a relief to him to know that everything would get done.

To my surprise, I didn't miss my city summer at all. After my chores I read outdoors in the pleasant weather. Breakfasts were not late and lazy, but I didn't mind. Instead, I looked forward to getting up and tending to the animals. I loved the gentle cows and the comical chickens.

When Mom and Dad visited on weekends, they were mystified by the change in me. At summer's end, I was both happy and sorry to go home.

The first morning back, I leapt out of bed at first light. Mom and Dad were very surprised.

"What would you like for breakfast, Heather?" Mom asked.

"Fresh bread!" I replied, remembering the wonderful smells in Grandma's kitchen.

"I'm afraid we're out of bread," Mom said, opening the breadbox. "Would you run to the store for a loaf?"

"No need," I said. "I know a better way!" I got out the flour.

Think About It

1. What are some ways Heather changes during her summer on the farm?

2. How would you feel about spending a summer with Heather's grandma? Tell why you feel that way.

3. After Heather has been on the farm for a few days, she writes to her friend Allison in the city. Write the note she sends.

A Friend in Need

by Jennifer Lien
illustrated by Ed Martinez

Nineteen-year-old Morris Frank of Nashville, Tennessee, felt fortunate. Unlike most others who were blind in the 1920s, he was attending college and working at a job. He could use a stylus and paper to transcribe his notes for both in Braille. He had many friends and was asked to lots of parties. One thing, however, caused him much frustration. Outgoing as he was, he could not go out alone. He always needed a friend or a paid guide to lead him.

One evening in 1927, Frank's father read aloud an article written by an American woman living in Switzerland. Dorothy Eustis wrote that dogs were being trained in Germany to guide people who had become blind in World War I. Frank became excited at what he heard. What a great idea! Maybe having a guide dog would be a workable approach to his problem.

Full of optimism, he wrote to Dorothy Eustis. If she would train him with a dog, he promised, he would help her start a program to help others.

Eustis invited Frank to come to Switzerland, but how would he get there? His mother, who was also blind, and his father, who owned a business, couldn't travel with him. Frank was shipped over by American Express.

Dorothy and George Eustis and another American, Jack Humphrey, had been breeding German shepherd dogs. They had been training them for police and rescue work. Before Morris Frank arrived, they traveled to Germany to learn how dogs were being trained to lead people who were blind.

In Switzerland, Frank was introduced to the beautiful female German shepherd who would share his life. Her name was Kiss, but Frank called her Buddy—a name the world would come to know.

Buddy was fitted with a harness to which a U-shaped handle was attached. Her trainers had devised this as a way for Frank to feel her movements. As they trained together, her signals gradually became more obvious to him.

Buddy had been educated, rather than simply trained. A guide dog must know when to refuse to do as it is asked. If the person who is blind gives the command "Forward," and a car is coming, the dog must not budge. Praise is the approach used to educate a guide dog.

When Morris Frank boarded the steamship to return home, the difference in him was obvious. With Buddy, he strode confidently about the decks. His new independence revived his spirit as his old frustrations blew away on the sea breeze.

When they arrived in New York, reporters looking for a news break wanted to put them to a test. Frank knew that it could be dangerous to enter New York traffic with a dog trained in a Swiss village. However, he decided the benefits to others outweighed the risks. He and Buddy had to prove that dogs could be guides for Americans who were blind. He knew that this was a workable idea that could simplify their lives.

His blood racing in his veins, Morris Frank gave the command to Buddy. "Forward!" The city roared around the two of them as they stepped off the curb. Frank concentrated on the signals coming to him through the handle connecting him to Buddy. He knew he had to trust his dog to get him safely across the street.

It probably took only eighteen or twenty seconds to cross. To the watching reporters, it felt like an age. Had they doomed the brave man and dog? When the pair made it, everyone's good spirits revived. On the sidewalk, Buddy stood calmly as trucks rumbled by. A dog that could handle New York traffic could obviously handle traffic anywhere.

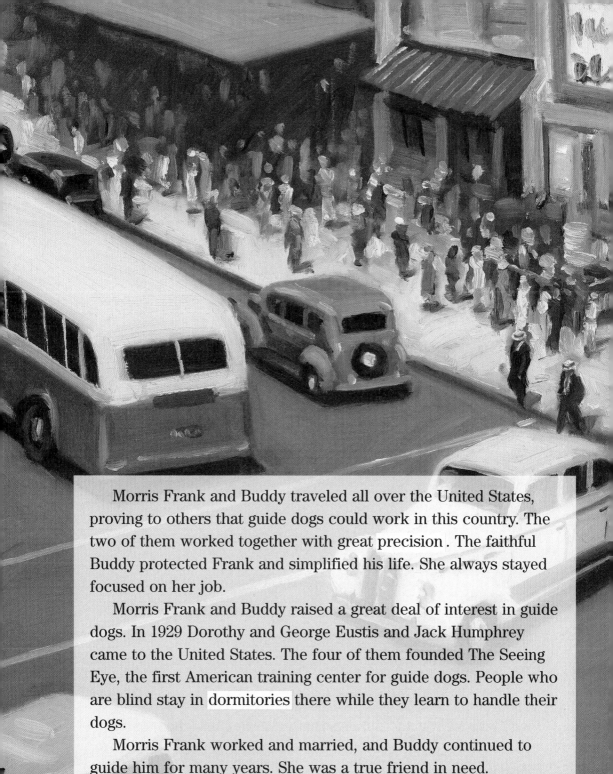

Morris Frank and Buddy traveled all over the United States, proving to others that guide dogs could work in this country. The two of them worked together with great precision. The faithful Buddy protected Frank and simplified his life. She always stayed focused on her job.

Morris Frank and Buddy raised a great deal of interest in guide dogs. In 1929 Dorothy and George Eustis and Jack Humphrey came to the United States. The four of them founded The Seeing Eye, the first American training center for guide dogs. People who are blind stay in dormitories there while they learn to handle their dogs.

Morris Frank worked and married, and Buddy continued to guide him for many years. She was a true friend in need.

Think About It

1. How did Buddy and Morris Frank change the lives of many Americans who are blind?

2. Do you think Morris Frank made a good decision when he let the reporters put him to the test on such a busy New York street? Explain.

3. Think about what you've learned about Morris Frank. Make a web with words and phrases that describe him. Then, using your web as a guide, write a descriptive paragraph about Morris Frank.

Our Best Friend

How do you stop a dog from barking in the backyard?
    Put him in the front yard.

Where can you leave your barking dog?
    In a barking lot.

When do dogs have eight legs?
    When there are two of them.

When the boy's dog was lost, why didn't he advertise
in the newspaper?
    Because he knew the dog couldn't read.

What did the dog say when its father had a bruised shoulder?
    "I have a sore pa."

How did dogs travel out West in pioneer days?
    In waggin' trains.

Sitting It Out

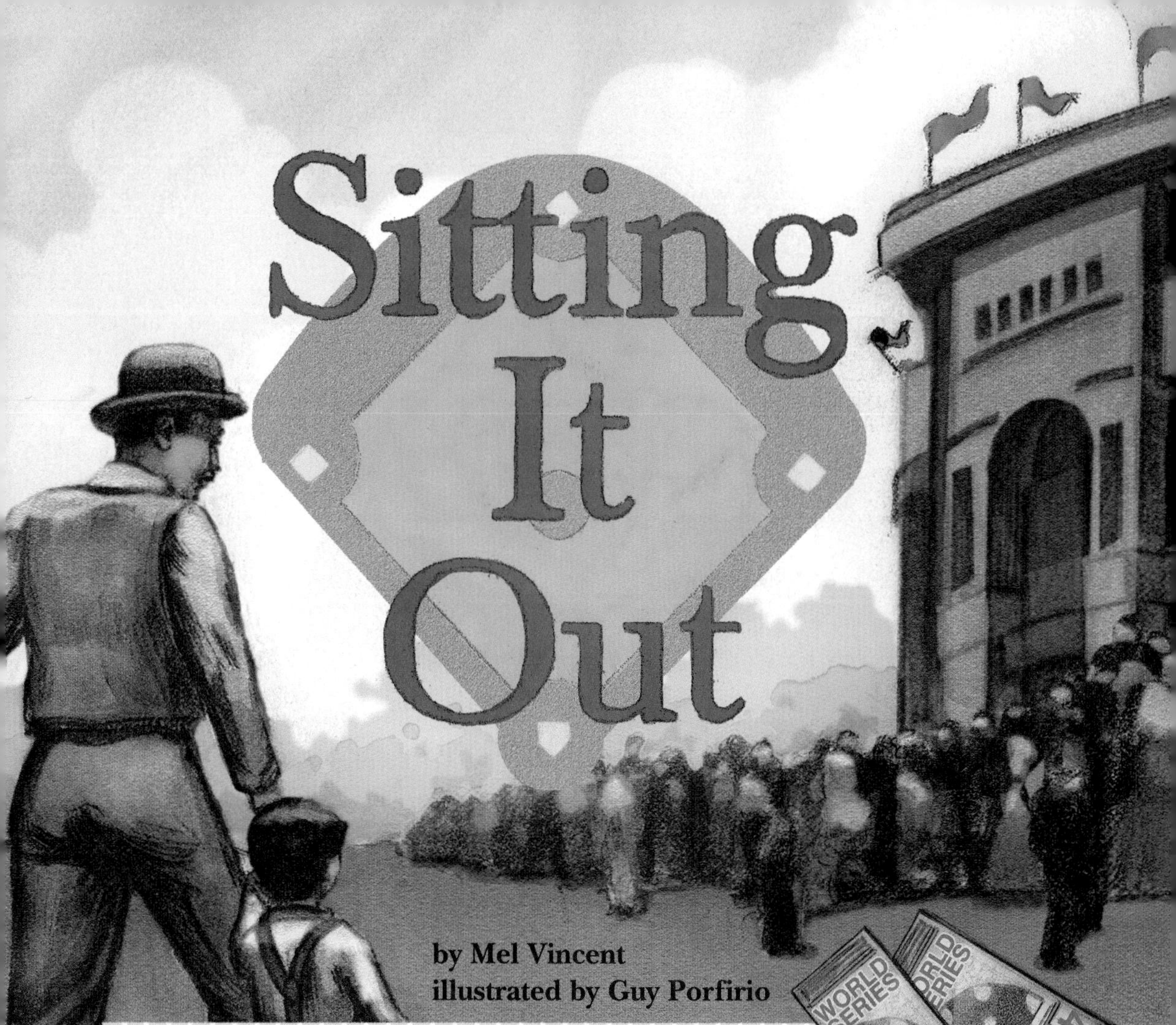

by Mel Vincent
illustrated by Guy Porfirio

CHARACTERS

JIM COOK, *age 14*

TOMMY DAVIS, *age 12*

BEN BERGER, *age 12*

BILLY TYLER, *age 13*

SUSIE TYLER, *age 5*

WORKER, *a worker at the ballpark*

SCENE 1

TIME: *October 11, 1906.*

SETTING: *Outside West Side Park, home of the Chicago Cubs. People who have bought tickets are headed for the gates. Today, game three of the World Series between the Cubs and the Chicago White Sox will be played.*

JIM *(Pointing):* That door marked *Visiting Team* is where we'll get in to see the game.

TOMMY *(Bewildered):* Are you goofy? There's a man outside the door. He's not going to let us through there.

JIM: Don't get into a fluster. I didn't say we were going into the clubhouse. Just follow me. We need to get acquainted with that man.

BEN: I don't see what good it will do, but we'll give it a try.

JIM: All right, then. Let's go! *(Ben and Tommy nod in agreement.)*

SCENE 2

TIME: *Same.*

SETTING: *At Visiting Team door.*

JIM: Say, Mister, when will we see the players going in?

WORKER: They're in there now, boys. The game will be starting soon.

JIM (*Dramatically*): Oh, no! We came all the way up here from 48th Street for the sublime thrill of seeing the White Sox in person. Now we're too late!

WORKER: Why don't you go to your seats and see them on the playing field?

JIM: We don't have enough money for tickets. We used it all up getting here. We thought this would be a unique opportunity to see the players up close.

WORKER: Imagine that! You boys came here with no prospect of seeing the game?

TOMMY (*Solemnly*): No prospect, Mister. Jim said we'd be able to see the players out here, though.

WORKER (*Teasing*): That was naughty of Jim! Well, I'm acquainted with some of the players. I imagine I can get you boys some tickets.

JIM: Our friend Billy isn't here yet. Can you get one for him, too?

WORKER: I'll do my best. Wait here. I'll see if the players have four extra tickets. (*He exits.*)

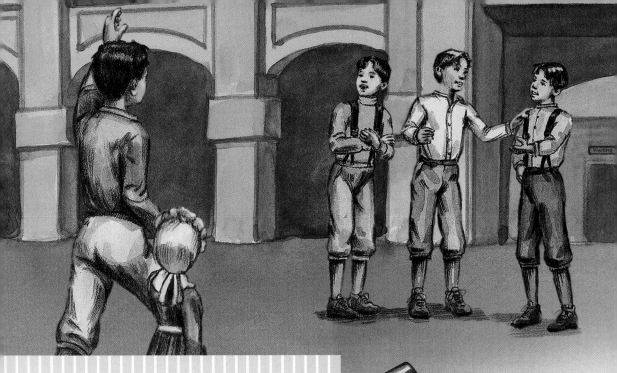

SCENE 3

TIME: *A little later.*

SETTING: *Same.*

JIM *(Displaying four tickets):* What did I tell you? I'm naughty, but my charm is irresistible! Now if our pal Billy would just show up, we could go inside and watch the game.

TOMMY: Keep your temper, Jim. Here comes Billy now. Uh-oh, he has Susie with him.

JIM: What! We don't have a ticket for his little sister!

BILLY *(Approaching sheepishly):* My mother said I couldn't go unless I brought her.

SUSIE *(Whining):* I'm thirsty.

JIM: Billy, this wrecks all our plans! We only have four tickets.

SUSIE *(In a temper):* I'm thirsty! Get me a drink or I'll tell Mama!

BILLY *(Displaying his frustration):* Okay, OKAY! We have to figure out how to get you inside first, though.

BEN: Susie can have my ticket.

TOMMY *(Puzzled):* Ben! You'll miss everything, and Susie doesn't know a thing about baseball.

BEN *(To Tommy):* Well, she can't wait outside by herself. Besides, Billy's a bigger White Sox fan than I am. I'll wait for you here. Maybe I'll see a player going home early.

BILLY: Thanks, Ben! If I get a foul ball, I'll give it to you.

SCENE 4

TIME: *A few hours later.*

SETTING: *At same Visiting Team door.
Ben has been talking to the worker.*

WORKER: That was a nice thing you did, sitting it out. I thought you
South Side boys were all tough.

BEN: We *are* tough!

WORKER *(Laughing):* Here come your friends. Don't go off yet. *(Exits)*

TOMMY *(Excitedly):* Big Ed Walsh shut them out!

WORKER: *(Appears and tosses ball to Ben):* This is for you, tough boy!

BEN: Wow! This ball is unique! It's signed by Big Ed Walsh!

JIM: Better hang on to that! Now we *all* had a good day!

Think About It

1. How do the boys get tickets to the third
   game of the World Series?

2. How do you think the worker feels about
   Ben and the other South Side boys? Why do
   you think that?

3. The worker writes a letter to a friend, telling
   about the South Side boys he met. Write the
   letter that the worker sends his friend.

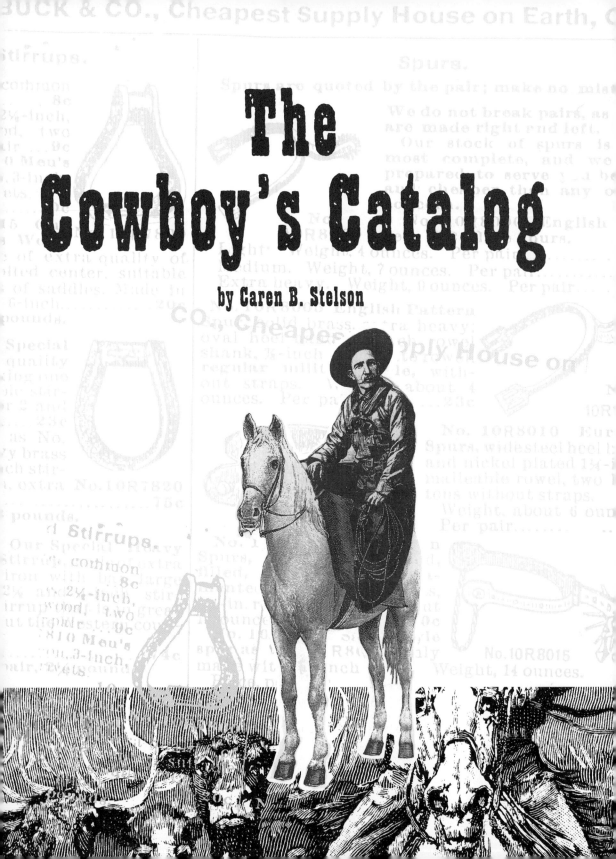

The Cowboy's Catalog

by Caren B. Stelson

Howdy Partner!

Looking for some new duds before you hit the trail? Then browse through this here wish book. We've got what you need to be a full-fledged cowpoke. If you're not satisfied with our merchandise, just holler, and we'll give you your money back, guaranteed. Partner, we're honest, and we aim to please. Order from us, and we'll make you as happy as a dog with two tails.

Long Johns

Hats

Shirts

Pants

Vests

Boots

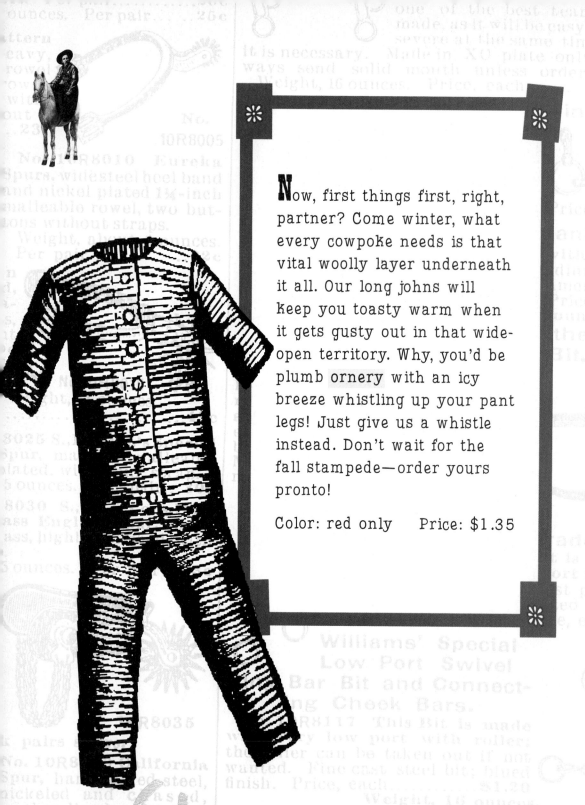

Now, first things first, right, partner? Come winter, what every cowpoke needs is that vital woolly layer underneath it all. Our long johns will keep you toasty warm when it gets gusty out in that wide-open territory. Why, you'd be plumb ornery with an icy breeze whistling up your pant legs! Just give us a whistle instead. Don't wait for the fall stampede—order yours pronto!

Color: red only   Price: $1.35

Every cowpoke up and down the Chisholm Trail knows that the Stetson hat is one vital piece of cowboy attire. It'll keep the sun off your scalp and the rain off your neck. When necessary, use it as a flyswatter or as a water bucket for your horse. Folks do say the smell of an old Stetson can permeate a room, but this hat will never fall apart. These days, the best-dressed cowpokes are favoring hats with fancy trims around the crown. We have the hat—you provide the trim. How about a nice rattlesnake? Only joking, partner!

Colors: black, brown, and gray   Price: $5.00

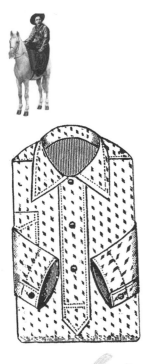

We know you don't like to be hog-tied with fancy words. Simply put, our shirts are the best you'll find this side of the Mississippi. Wool or cotton, in a check, print, or stripe, our shirts are all as tough as tumbleweeds. Don't go asking us for red, though. Red will make even the calmest cows ornery. In a red shirt, you'll have a stampede on your hands! In our shirts, you'll have cattle that are tranquil and compliant. They'll just mosey along as sweet as you please.

Colors: drab gray or blue   Price: $.85

When it comes to work pants, we sell only the toughest. They're made from "shrink-to-fit" denim cloth. Jump in a horse trough, dry out, and they'll be a perfect fit. We know you ride over rough, craggy terrain twelve hours a day out in sagebrush territory. These jeans will stand up to the worst punishment you can give them. Miners say they're worth their weight in gold. Why not add some new leather chaps, too? You'll look good in the saddle until the very last cow is corralled at the end of the trail.

Pants: $.75   Chaps: $1.25

Unless you're a plain greenhorn, you know you've got to have a vest. Everyone needs a little diversion for those tranquil evenings by the campfire. Whichever one you favor—whittling, playing harmonica, writing in a diary—our vest has a pocket for it. While you're at it, order up a dozen new Turkey Red bandannas. How else will you keep from eating dust? Use them to shade your neck, mop your brow, and polish your boots, too!

Vest: $1.00   Bandannas: $.30/dozen

You'll be grinning like a possum when you slide your feet into a pair of these beauties. Seventeen inches tall, these boots will protect your legs from sharp thorns in cactus terrain. We give you an extra inch in the heel. Helps your foot stay in the stirrup and adds a little extra height when you amble into town. You know you need some new boots. Order from us, and we'll have you riding tall in the saddle.

Price: $3.00 No half-sizes.
For best fit, order
one size smaller.

Think About It

1. What is the most expensive item a cowboy could order from the catalog? What is the least expensive item?

2. The catalog warns that in a red shirt, "you'll have a stampede on your hands." Why, then, do you think it offers red bandannas and red long johns?

3. If you were a cowpoke, what would you want to order from the Cowboy's Catalog? Write a letter ordering at least three items. Remember to include information about size, color, and price.

Great Shakes!

by Meish Goldish

Red-hot lava shoots out of this volcano. Some eruptions produce clouds of hot ash.

If you think volcanoes and earthquakes threaten only distant lands, it's time to do some rethinking. Parts of the North American continent, including the United States, have to worry about volcanoes and earthquakes, too.

In some countries, volcanic eruptions have submerged entire islands. Earthquakes have taken hundreds of thousands of lives. The United States has not had such extensive losses, but there have been several tragic events.

One morning in April 1906, an unexpected earthquake rocked San Francisco. The ground shook hard for about a minute, stopped briefly, and then restarted.

Many fires broke out when gas lamps fell and gas stoves exploded. Firefighters were unable to cope because the underground water pipes were damaged. Flames raged for three days before they were finally controlled. In all, about 700 people died and 300,000 others lost their homes. Some 28,000 buildings were destroyed.

The buildings on the left side of the picture lean after the 1906 San Francisco earthquake. Those on the right side seem unharmed. Across the street, only rubble remains.

The people of San Francisco rebuilt as quickly as possible. They hoped no more major earthquakes would hit their city. Unfortunately, this hope could not last.

In October 1989, another terrible earthquake hit San Francisco. This one happened in the late afternoon, as people were returning home from work. Roads and highways broke up and disconnected, causing cars to collide. Buildings swayed and crashed to the ground.

The 1989 San Francisco earthquake caused this highway to collapse.

This scientist uses special equipment
to read movements within the earth.

Unlike the earthquake of 1906, this one lasted
only about 15 seconds. When it was over, people
reacted to the damage with shock and disbelief.
Not only had 63 people died, more than 100,000
homes were in disrepair. How could such an event
have come upon the city unannounced?

The fact is that researchers can't yet tell exactly
when and where an earthquake will strike. However,
they are studying every microscopic movement of
the earth to learn more.

Mount St. Helens erupted in 1980,
spewing ash and smoke into the air.

The traditional image of an active volcano is of one on a
faraway tropical island. Perhaps because of this, a volcano on
our own continent caught Washington State unprepared.

Mount St. Helens had been quiet since 1857, causing some
to think it was extinct. In May 1980 it erupted unexpectedly.
Molten rock and hot ash rushed up the cylinder-shaped
shaft inside and shot into the air. Much of the forest on the
mountain burned. Sixty people died, as well as thousands
of animals and plants.

Not everyone had been unaware of the coming disaster. Days before the blast, a warning had appeared. A transparent veil of smoke had risen from the top of the mountain. It was a sign that molten rock inside was ready to erupt.

Before the blast, roads to Mount St. Helens were closed, and people living nearby moved away. This was wise. The volcano's heat melted the snow on the mountain, causing floods and mudslides. Homes and crops were destroyed, but thanks to good planning, many lives were saved.

The eruption left Mount St. Helens with an enormous crater.

Think About It

1. What types of damage do earthquakes and volcanoes cause?

2. Why do you think people choose to live in places where earthquakes are common?

3. Imagine feeling an earthquake or watching a volcano erupt. Write a story about the experience.

In 1995 the city of Kobe, Japan, was hit by a very destructive earthquake.

Pick the Right One

Chances are you can spell the name of our planet. It wasn't always spelled *earth*, though. This word was *erthe* in Middle English and, before that, *eorthe* in Old English. Can you guess the meaning of each of these "earth" words? Answers are at the bottom of the page.

Do you think an *earthnut* is someone who cares deeply about conserving natural resources or the edible nutlike, underground part of a plant?

Do you suppose *earthrise* is a hill or mountain, or the rise of Earth above the moon's horizon?

Which is called *earthstar*—a type of fungus, or a recently discovered star in the constellation Orion that resembles Earth?

How about *earthenware*? Is it clothing made of natural materials, or dishes made of clay?

Answers: second choice, second choice, first choice, second choice

213

FINDING THE TITANIC

by Meish Goldish   illustrated by Matt Straub

In 1912, the *Titanic* proudly set sail from England to New York on its first voyage. Excitement abounded among the 2,200 passengers and crew members on board.

In the realm of steamships, the *Titanic* was considered the finest ever constructed. It was the largest and fanciest liner in existence. People hailed it as the ship that was impossible to sink.

Then the unexpected happened. In the middle of the night, after four days at sea, the *Titanic* struck an iceberg.

At first, passengers disregarded the seemingly harmless incident. After all, the ship was said to have great buoyancy. However, after the crew had fully inspected the damage, the happy mood on board dissipated. It was quickly replaced by panic and terror as the *Titanic* slowly began to sink. All realized that it would soon slip below the surface.

No plans had been made for such an emergency. There were not enough lifeboats for all to escape. As a result, more than 1,500 people died that night in the icy sea.

For 73 years, the *Titanic* lay quietly on the sea floor, miles below the surface. Then, in 1985, a team of French and American explorers set out to find the sunken ship.

Using sonar and video instruments, the team searched carefully for six long weeks. Storms were brewing at sea, so their search time was running out. Even using a diversity of video and acoustic equipment, they could find no sign of the *Titanic*. Was locating the lost ship simply impossible?

Finally, on one of the last days left, an image suddenly appeared on a video monitor. It was a boiler from the *Titanic*! Soon other items from the sunken ship came into view on the screen. The explorers cheered loudly, knowing they had at last discovered the wreck. A depth gauge showed that the *Titanic* lay two and one-half miles beneath the surface.

Team members quickly took photos of the wreckage. Then they headed to shore to escape the coming storms.

For months, the explorers planned a return trip to examine the *Titanic* at closer range. They agreed that it would be improper to salvage any of the wreckage. Their aim was simply to learn exactly how and why the great ship sank.

In 1986 the team returned with a sonar-equipped submersible and a remote-controlled underwater robot. This time the explorers were able to head directly to where the wreck lay.

ALVIN

Inside the submersible, named *Alvin*, team members were able to study the *Titanic* up close. They observed the effects of its long underwater existence. They also confirmed that the ship had broken into two pieces before sinking.

In 1987 a different team of explorers visited the *Titanic* and brought up some of its remains. However, Congress soon passed a law ordering that the *Titanic* be left undisturbed. Most people agree it would be heartless indeed to show disrespect to the victims of this awful tragedy.

Think About It

1. How did using modern equipment make it possible to find the *Titanic*?

2. How difficult do you think it would be to bring up the remains of the *Titanic*? Explain your answer.

3. You are a member of the team that finally finds the *Titanic*. Write a journal entry about that exciting event.

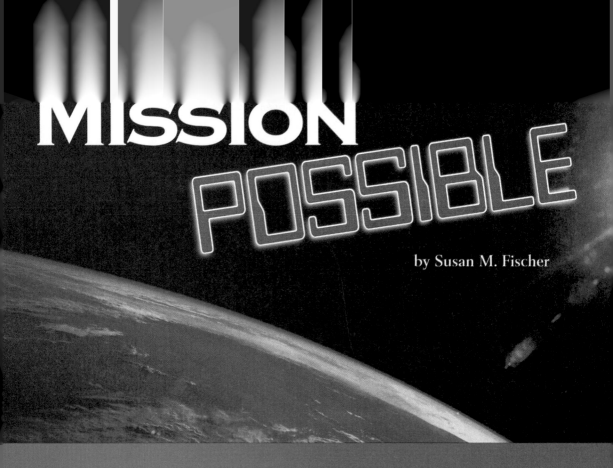

MISSION POSSIBLE

by Susan M. Fischer

Thousands of years ago, it would have been impossible for the people then living to predict space travel. As time passed, humans gazed at the sky and began to experiment. Rockets, for example, were invented hundreds of years ago. However, it was only recently that people discovered how to get a rocket into space.

On April 12, 1961, Yuri Gagarin of the Soviet Union became the first person in space. A powerful rocket launched him high enough for one orbit around Earth. This amazing achievement by the Soviet Union presented a challenge to the United States space program.

"...A PLEASANT RIDE..."

The next month, on May 5, 1961, astronaut Alan Shepard became the first American in space. A six-story-high Mercury-Redstone rocket launched the space capsule he rode in, the *Freedom VII*. Although the historic flight lasted only fifteen minutes, it was a milestone for the United States.

Commander Shepard's duties during the flight were to analyze his responses, to maneuver the spacecraft with high-tech controls, and to survive! He returned to Earth safely as an American hero. Asked to describe his trip and the weightlessness he experienced beyond Earth's gravity, he called it "just a pleasant ride."

Alan Shepard

"...ONE GIANT LEAP..."

    With the success of *Freedom VII*, President John F. Kennedy set a bold new goal for the space program. He announced that the United States would land an astronaut on the moon before 1970. The *Apollo* Space Mission was underway!

    On July 16, 1969, *Apollo 11* was launched from the Kennedy Space Center's facilities. Four days later, on July 20, 1969, astronauts Edwin "Buzz" Aldrin and Neil Armstrong became the first humans to set foot on the moon. All the world watched on TV as Armstrong stepped off the ladder of the *Eagle*, the small landing craft. As his boot touched the surface of the moon, he spoke his historic words. "That's one small step for a man, one giant leap for mankind."

Neil Armstrong

exploring Mars

The exploring of space didn't end with the moon landing. The space program turned to navigation among the planets of our solar system. In 1975 NASA launched two uncrewed *Viking* missions to Earth's neighbor, Mars.

The goal of the *Viking* mission was to determine whether simple forms of life existed on Mars. In 1976, after about a year of travel each, the two *Viking* orbiters reached Mars. They immediately began sending back photographs to Earth. Both orbiters also sent down landers, which survived the impact and took soil samples. The soil of Mars was analyzed in the landers' labs and the results were beamed to specialists.

NASA scientists found only nonliving materials on Mars. However, what they learned makes them believe that exploring by humans will one day be possible there.

The *Voyager* missions were also uncrewed. They were designed to explore the outer planets—Jupiter, Saturn, Uranus, Neptune, and Pluto.

Launched in 1977, *Voyager 2* visited all of these planets. From photographs it sent back, scientists made amazing discoveries about each. In 1986 the data it beamed to Earth showed that Uranus had ten rings. In 1989 it revealed that Neptune had several more rings than scientists thought and many moons.

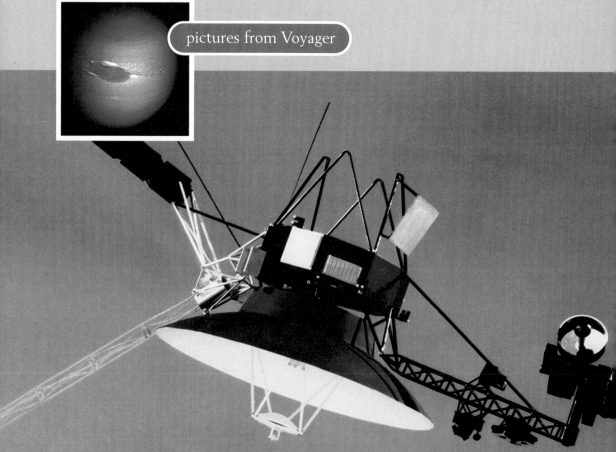

pictures from Voyager

Guion Bluford

Sally Ride

In 1983, mission specialist Sally Ride became the first American woman in space. In the same year, Guion Bluford became the first African American in space. Both flew on the shuttle *Challenger*, as did Bruce McCandless. In 1984 McCandless was the first to spacewalk without a lifeline, using the rocket-powered maneuvering unit.

Sadly, disaster struck the space program in 1986, when the *Challenger* exploded. The whole world was saddened by this tragic accident.

Putting the *Challenger* accident behind them, American astronauts continue to train for the space program. They take part in flight simulations to prepare for the weightlessness of zero gravity. Then they rocket into space on new and exciting missions. Someday these missions will take the people of Earth far beyond their own moon.

Think About It

1. What country had the first person in space? How did this space flight affect the American space program?

2. Why do you think "all the world watched on TV" when astronauts Aldrin and Armstrong became the first humans to set foot on the moon?

3. Think about cosmonaut Yuri Gagarin when he was about to become the first person in space. What do you think he thought and felt as the rocket was about to blast off? Write about his thoughts and feelings.

That's What He Said!

"It's nearly impossible to breathe inside this spacecraft," Tom said stuffily.

"It looks cold out there in space," Tom said frostily.

"Wool socks would feel good," Tom said sheepishly.

"We should have brought the camera with the preloaded film," Tom said snappily.

"I can't tell which way to point the camera," Tom said aimlessly.

"I'm hungry. I could use a big plate of spaghetti," Tom said saucily.

"We're out of lemonade," Tom said sourly.

"I'd like some beef jerky," Tom said dryly.

"We've been on this mission for seven days," Tom said weakly.

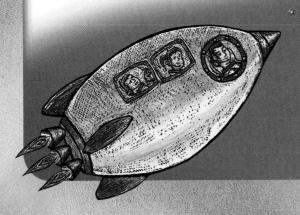

229

UNTANGLING the WEB

Help! I'm caught in an electronic web!

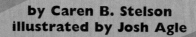

by Caren B. Stelson
illustrated by Josh Agle

Never fear—Super Spider is here! I got your message, Newbie, and I came as fast as I could. Yep, just as I thought. You're tangled in the biggest web in the world—the World Wide Web. Don't worry, we'll get you free. Here's how we'll do it. You wiggle a finger out and type me a question on your keyboard. I'll answer your questions, and together we'll get you untangled!

What *is* the World Wide Web anyway?

What is the World Wide Web anyway?

Good question, Newbie. The World Wide Web, or "the Web" for short, is a gigantic collection of computer files. These electronic files, called Web sites, are linked together all over the world. The transmission of these files is handled by your computer modem. The modem is a piece of interactive equipment that lets your computer communicate with other computers. It does this by sending codes over the phone lines.

What can I use the Web for?

ASTRONAUTS

FRIENDS

Newbie, you'll be amazed at all the interesting information you can find on the Web. All you have to do is choose a general subject or a specific destination. Want to learn about astronauts? Hop online, and go to the Air and Space Museum's Web site in Washington, D.C. Interested in French paintings? Go to the Louvre Museum's Web site in Paris. Wondering what's happening around your own town? Your science museum, your school, and even your best friend may have a Web site for you to explore. The possibilities are endless.

What can I use the Web for?

SCHOOL

PARIS

Well, Newbie, it works like this. You start with a powerful program in your computer called a Web browser. The browser is what takes you where you want to go on the World Wide Web. Any Web site you want to visit has an electronic address. You just type in the address, and the browser finds your desired destination. A Web site address may look like a strange string of letters, dots, and slashes to you. Your Web browser, however, recognizes the format and takes you to the correct site instantly—well, almost!

Web Browser

MUSEUMS

What if I don't know the Web site address?

When you don't know the exact Web site address, you can use something called a search engine. A search engine looks for Web sites about the topic you want to explore. To use the search engine, you type in words about your topic and click "SEARCH." The search engine displays a list of all the sites that contain the words you typed.

Certain words in the listings the search engine provides may be in a different color. These words are hypertext links to other sites. If you want information about astronauts, you just click on hypertext that has to do with astronauts. Some search engines will also give you a brief summary of each site. That helps you identify the ones that are likely to be useful.

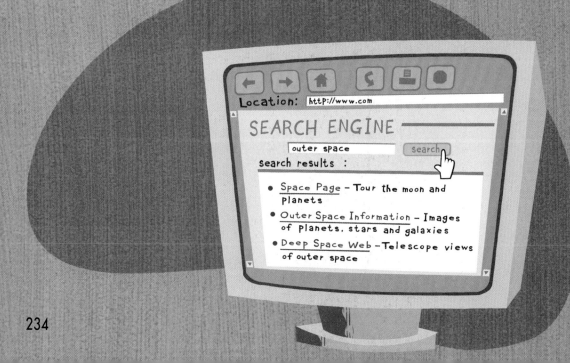

Super Spider, I've been wondering— what is e-mail?

What is e-mail?

One of the most popular things to do on the Web is send electronic mail, or e-mail for short. With the help of your modem, you can send e-mail to anyone who has an e-mail address.

An e-mail letter is a lot like a regular letter, but its format is a little different. The **To** line is for the address of the person who is to receive your message. The **From** line is for the address of the person sending the message—you! The **Subject** line tells briefly what the message is about. The **Message** is the body of the letter.

Sending e-mail is easy. You just compose your message, carefully type in the address of the person you're sending it to, and click "SEND." In a short time, that person receives your electronic letter.

Now can I start exploring the World Wide Web on my own?

Before you start out, Newbie, remember this. A popular Web site sometimes gets bombarded with "hits." This happens when too many people try to use it at once. The barrage of signals can mean a delay for you. If you can't get to a Web site, just try again later.

Remember this, too. Using the World Wide Web is a lot like traveling in the real world. It's exciting, but you have to be careful. Make sure you never give out credit card numbers or personal information over the Web. If you should find yourself at a Web site that's not for kids, LEAVE IT at once!

Okay, Newbie, we did it! We've got you untangled and ready to explore the Web. Have fun!

Think About It

1. What is the World Wide Web? What kinds of information can you find on the Web?

2. What is hypertext? Why is it helpful?

3. Newbie spends some time exploring the Web. Then he sends Super Spider another message, telling what he has done and what he thinks of the Web. Write the message Newbie sends.

Cindy "Science" Spots

by Mary Wright   illustrated by Debra Spina-Dixon

Cindy "Science" Vincent jumped onto her bike and headed for her friend Gene's house. It wasn't far, and she often walked. Today, however, she was excited about her new computer and couldn't wait to tell Gene about it. She planned to use it to do her space research on the Internet.

Cindy parked her bicycle by the fence and rang the doorbell. When Gene opened the door, he was already talking excitedly. "Cindy, there's a man here you've got to meet! My dad might give him a job at the lab where he works."

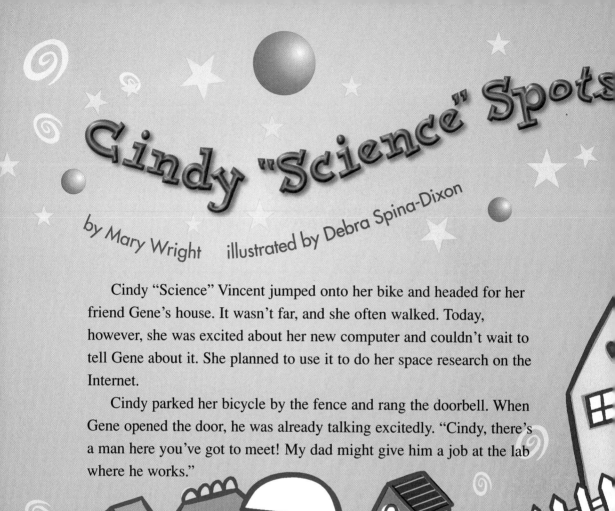

the Clues

"I came over to tell you about my new computer," Cindy began. "I found a Web site for my research on plant cells in space. The experts there say . . ."

"This man was a real cosmonaut!" Cyrus broke in. "He orbited the sun with our astronauts and . . ."

"He orbited the sun? I don't think so! No one's ever done that."

"Maybe it was a star or something. Anyway, come and meet him."

239

Inside, Cindy met Professor Durak, standing in the center of the family room. "Good to meet you, Cindy," he said. "I was just talking about the breakthrough I made for space science back in 1969."

Gene's dad smiled. "Our neighbor Cindy is an expert on space science, Professor Durak. She plans to make it her career."

"She enrolls in Space Camp every summer," Gene put in.

John Glenn Neil Armstrong
Buzz Aldrin
Thanks for all your
help, Prof. July, 1999

Professor Durak gave Cindy a sharp look. "The experts disregarded my formulas in planning our flight. The launch was rough, and I had to teach the astronauts how to correct it. They were grateful enough to honor me by signing this shirt after the flight."

"What happened with the launch?" Gene asked.

"The spacecraft didn't take off properly," said Professor Durak. "The astronauts had no idea what to do, but my knowledge saved the day."

Cindy listened with careful attention.

"As our craft rose through the atmosphere, we watched the altimeter numbers rise. At eight thousand feet, we passed a satellite. Once we had left Earth's atmosphere, ah, that was a sight to see."

"What was?" Cindy asked.

"Seeing the planets from space, of course. Mars, the red planet! Jupiter, with its ring! Venus, with its Great Red Spot!"

Gene whistled in amazement, but Cindy nudged him and began to cough. "Gene," she croaked, pointing to the kitchen, "would you get me some juice?"

When they got there, Cindy's coughing turned to laughter.

"Professor Durak is a fake, Gene!" she said. "I hope your father hasn't taken any action yet about giving him a job."

Gene sighed dejectedly. "You're awesome when it comes to space facts, so you're probably right. But how do you know Professor Durak's a fake?"

"There are three clues. First, look closely at the professor's shirt. Next, read about Jupiter in a book or online."

Can YOU spot Professor Durak's mistakes? Look up spaceflight dates and crews in an almanac. Then check out Jupiter.

Answer: The professor said his flight was in 1969, but the writing on his shirt says 1999. John Glenn, Neil Armstrong, and Buzz Aldrin were never on a mission together. The Great Red Spot is on Jupiter. It's an immense hurricane that was first seen in 1664.

Think About It

1. Why does Cindy say that she hopes Gene's father has not given Professor Durak a job?

2. How do you think Professor Durak feels about meeting Cindy?

3. Think about Cindy "Science" Vincent. Make a web with words that tell about her interests and the things she does. Then write a paragraph describing Cindy.